Oracle Scripts

Oracle Scripts

Brian Lomasky and David C. Kreines

O'REILLY™

Beijing · Cambridge · Köln · Paris · Sebastopol · Taipei · Tokyo

Oracle Scripts

by Brian Lomasky and David C. Kreines

Copyright © 1998 O'Reilly & Associates, Inc. All rights reserved.
Printed in the United States of America.

Published by O'Reilly & Associates, Inc., 101 Morris Street, Sebastopol, CA 95472.

Editor: Deborah Russell

Production Editor: John Files

Printing History:

April 1998:   First Edition.

This book is printed on acid-free paper with 85% recycled content, 15% post-consumer waste. O'Reilly & Associates is committed to using paper with the highest recycled content available consistent with high quality.

ISBN: 1-56592-438-X   [12/98]

For Anne, who allowed me the time to create this book.

—Brian Lomasky

For my wife Suzanne, for always being there to carry the load.

—David C. Kreines

Table of Contents

Preface

Everybody should believe in something.
I believe I'll go fishing.
—Henry David Thoreau

This is a book for Oracle database administrators (DBAs) and developers. So you might immediately ask: "What does a quote about fishing have to do with database administration?" Well, for the typical Oracle professional, fishing (or almost any other leisure activity, for that matter) is usually out of the question. By definition, the DBA bears full responsibility for the proper operation of the Oracle databases under his or her control. As long as the database performs up to expectations and nothing goes wrong, everyone is happy and thinks you're doing a great job. But in the real world where we live, things do go wrong, and the database does not always perform the way we wish it would; in such cases, it's the DBA's problem. Every DBA recognizes this enigma: nobody even knows you exist until something goes wrong, and then you are responsible for everything!

Developers are not exempt from the pressures of time and expectations either. The typical developer (even with the most modern set of GUI tools and support from the best DBAs) is faced with increased workloads, longer backlogs, and a general expectation that more be accomplished faster.

Are we being a bit melodramatic? Perhaps. However, the purpose of this book is to make life easier for Oracle DBAs and developers by providing a tried and true set of tools that will automate many of your required tasks and allow you to keep that database running at the peak of perfection. We also provide tools to help the developer automate some of the more common functions and to get information from the Oracle data dictionary quickly and easily. And when things don't go exactly right, we provide the tools you need to diagnose and repair the problem with a minimum amount of disruption. In the end, this means that you *will* have time to go fishing!

Oracle DBAs (and, to a lesser extent, developers as well) are faced with a variety of ongoing tasks, including monitoring the Oracle databases for continuous reliability, performance, and security issues. Oracle Corporation provides a variety of internal views of the database that may be used by the DBA to gather and summarize data in order to create the desired reports. These views include:

- The DBA_ views
- The X$ tables
- The V$ views

The DBA typically builds queries and reports that utilize these views to provide insight into the internal workings of the database. These scripts, created in SQL or PL/SQL, allow the DBA to easily run their frequently-executed queries.

Four common problems are encountered when using this approach:

1. Since the same critical database information is usually required at every Oracle installation, DBAs seem to have reinvented an endless variety of what are essentially the same scripts—without benefit of each other's knowledge and experience.

2. Manually created scripts can contain typographical or logic errors. Such errors can cause scripts to fail or (even worse) execute without an error but produce incorrect output—output that the DBA may inadvertently rely for critical decision making.

3. DBAs do not typically have the luxury of sufficient free time in which to research and create complex scripts for managing their databases. Critical data may not be provided because the DBA hasn't had the time to implement a script feature.

4. There is no universal resource of previously created, documented, and tested scripts. While isolated examples of scripts do exist in a variety of places, such as user group archives, Internet repositories, etc., these scripts are often incomplete or inconsistent in architecture and output format.

In addition, Oracle databases run on host servers that operate in a variety of operating system environments. Oracle database operations can and do impact the performance of the operating system, especially the UNIX operating system. Likewise, no amount of Oracle database tuning can correct a problem that is rooted in the configuration of the operating system. This interaction, then, results in two more problems:

1. Most Oracle DBAs know very little about the operating system. The typical operating system administrator is too busy to devote much time to addressing database issues, and it's usually quite difficult to convince corporate manage-

ment to provide sufficient system administrator training for the Oracle DBA ("because that's the system administrator's job, not the Oracle DBA's job"). Besides, the DBA is too busy working with the database to worry about the operating system.

2. Most system administrators know very little about the Oracle database, since they're usually too busy with traditional operating system management duties, and have little time to comprehensively install, configure, and tune an Oracle database.

Unfortunately, since proper Oracle database configuration and performance depends on the proper configuration and performance of the operating system, this means that many systems are not optimally tuned.

Are there solutions to the problems we have identified? We think so, and that's why we wrote this book!

Structure of This Book

To make the most of this book and the scripts on the accompanying CD-ROM, you'll find it helpful to understand how the book is organized, and where to find what you need. This book is divided into five parts:

Part I : Overview

Chapter 1, *Introduction*, introduces the scripts, explains how to install them in your system, and describes how to use both the scripts and their accompanying documentation. It also contains a cross-reference listing showing all of the scripts provided with this book, along with a brief description of their functions.

Part II: Scripts for DBAs

This part contains chapters describing scripts aimed primarily at database administrators. The scripts provide a number of control and monitoring tools required for the day-to-day operation and support of a modern Oracle database.

Chapter 2, *Database Control Utilities*. These scripts allow the DBA to easily start up, shut down, and check the status of the Oracle database or SQL*Net.

Chapter 3, *Database Performance and Trend Analysis Utilities*. These scripts can be used to analyze the performance of the currently-executing SQL statements, report on ROLLBACK statements and wait statistics, and display overall Oracle database tuning metrics. UNIX system performance is measured by scripts that take a snapshot of the current system's performance metrics, and by a set of scripts that collect ongoing UNIX system performance statistics and then print a report of the bucketed performance data.

Chapter 4, *Database Reliability Monitoring Utilities*. These utilities analyze the alert log for redo log statistics and errors, monitor the database for any trace dump files that are created, display comprehensive locking information, search for and report on core dump files, and validate the structure of the database tables and indexes.

Chapter 5, *Database Security Reports and Utilities*. These scripts create various security reports used for database grants, profiles, quotas, roles, and user accounts. Over time, you can use these scripts to easily create auditing reports by user and object. You can also easily duplicate user accounts and create OPS$ accounts.

Chapter 6, *Database Backup Utilities*. These tools allow the DBA to perform an automatic cold or hot backup of an Oracle database. Database restoration scripts are automatically generated and included with the backup files. You will find it easy to integrate links to third-party UNIX backup tools into these scripts.

Chapter 7, *Oracle Applications Utilities*. These scripts, intended for use with the Oracle Applications, return the status of the concurrent manager process, and start or stop the concurrent managers for a given database.

Part III: Scripts for Developers and Designers

This part of the book contains chapters describing scripts that will be useful to those who are designing and developing Oracle databases and application programs, as well as to the DBAs who must support these systems.

Chapter 8, *Database-Design/DDL Utilities*. These scripts allow you to easily create, analyze, report, or reverse-engineer any of the objects in the database.

Chapter 9, *Database Developer Utilities*. These scripts allow the application developer or DBA to easily create EXPLAIN PLAN reports of SQL statements. This chapter also includes a set of easy-to-use front-end scripts for using RCS (Revision Control System) to manage source code.

Part IV: UNIX Utility Scripts

This part of the book contains chapters describing scripts that perform UNIX-level functions that both Oracle DBAs and developers will find helpful. Many of these scripts are also called by other scripts in this book.

Chapter 10, *General System Utilities*. This chapter contains a set of general common-purpose utilities that perform a variety of functions, including automatically logging off Oracle users, determining the operating system type, killing UNIX processes, and other useful UNIX-level activities.

Chapter 11, *Directory and File Management Utilities*. These scripts are provided to copy and compress files, define required parameters for DBA-related scripts, define a temporary scratch file name, restore and uncompress files, and calculate when a file was created.

Chapter 12, *Memory Usage Reports*. This chapter contains scripts that display all of the memory statistics for an HP-UX computer system, and display the amount of available free system memory (for Sun or HP-UX systems). You can easily customize them for your own environment.

Part V: Appendixes

The appendixes contain a series of summary tables.

Appendix A, *SQL Scripts That Create Oracle Tables*, lists the SQL scripts in the book, cross-referenced to the Oracle tables they create.

Appendix B, *Oracle Tables Created by SQL Scripts*, is the complement of Appendix A; it lists the Oracle tables created by SQL scripts, cross-referenced to those scripts.

Appendix C, *SQL Scripts That Create Output Files*, lists the SQL scripts in the book, cross-referenced to the output files they create.

Appendix D, *Output Files Created by SQL Scripts*, is the complement of Appendix C; it lists the output files created by SQL scripts, cross-referenced to those scripts.

Conventions Used in This Book

The following conventions are used in this book:

Italic
   Used for script, file, and directory names.

`Constant width`
   Used for code examples.

`Constant width italic`
   In some code examples, indicates an element (e.g., a parameter) that you supply.

[ ] In syntax descriptions, square brackets enclose optional items.

Platforms and Versions of Oracle

Most of the scripts described in this book were developed on a UNIX operating system; however, typically the scripts can be transferred readily to other operating systems, such as Windows NT. See the section "Converting to Other Operating

Systems" in Chapter 1, as well as the comments in the scripts themselves. The SQL scripts are particularly portable; most of these scripts will run as is on any operating system.

Most of the scripts also work with most versions of Oracle, from Oracle 7.x (and, in many cases, earlier) through Oracle 8.0.4 (and beyond).

About the CD-ROM

The CD-ROM included with this book contains all of the scripts described in the following chapters. The scripts are organized according to the following basic directory structure:

DBA
> Contains scripts that are generally useful to the DBA.

TOOLS
> Contains the rest of the scripts, which are generally useful to both DBAs and developers.

For your convenience, several additional files have been included to make it easier to copy the scripts:

dba.tar
> Contains all files for the DBA directory in standard UNIX tar format.

tools.tar
> Contains all files for the TOOLS directory in standard UNIX tar format.

dba.zip
> Contains all files for the DBA directory in zipped format.

tools.zip
> Contains all files for the TOOLS directory in zipped format.

In addition to the script files, you will find two pieces of software on the CD-ROM:

winzip95.exe
> An executable file containing a shareware version of the WinZIP product from Nico Mak Computing, Inc. We've provided this program in case you need it for unzipping the zip files included on the CD-ROM. Ordering and support information is provided in the file.

q
> A directory containing the files for Q, a full-use trial copy of the Q Diagnostic Center for Oracle and the PC from Savant Corporation. Q is designed to help DBAs and developers address performance tuning, problem diagnosis, and space management issues in networked Oracle environments. You can learn

more about Savant Corporation and the Q product family by visiting *www.savant-corp.com.* To obtain a key to use the trial version of Q, call Savant at 800-956-9541 or 301-581-0500. Technical support for Q is available at 301-581-0504 or by email at *qsupport@savant-corp.com.*

TIP   Savant Corporation recommends that to install Q you have at least
            32 megabytes of memory.

For installation instructions, see "Installing the Scripts" in Chapter 1, and the *readme.txt* file on the CD-ROM.

Comments and Questions

Please address comments and questions concerning this book to the publisher:

O'Reilly & Associates, Inc.
101 Morris Street
Sebastopol, CA 95472
800-998-9938 (in the U.S. or Canada)
707-829-0515 (international or local)
707-829-0104 (fax)

You can also send us messages electronically. For corrections and amplifications for the book and its accompanying CD-ROM, check out *www.oreilly.com/catalog/ oraclescrp.* See the ads at the end of the book for information about all of O'Reilly & Associates' online services.

For the WinZIP product, address questions and comments to Nico Mak Computing; for the Q product, address Savant Corporation. See "About the CD-ROM" for contact information.

Acknowledgments

We are in debt to many people who have helped (intentionally or not) to make this book possible. Much of our collective knowledge is due in large part to interactions with a universe of incredibly talented professionals. In particular, the many members of the International Oracle Users Group—Americas, as well as many other Oracle users around the world have contributed more than they may ever know to the collective knowledge of the Oracle community. The staff members of Oracle Corporation, in general, and Oracle Support in particular, also deserve our appreciation for a wealth of information shared.

This book would not be possible without an incredible amount of hard work and dedication by the staff of O'Reilly & Associates. In particular, we want to thank our editor, Debby Russell, who handled the very tight production schedule for this book by alternately prodding and encouraging us and doing whatever it took to get the job done. Special thanks to John Dockery, without whose invaluable assistance this book would not have come to fruition. Thanks as well to John Files, the production editor; Mary Jennifer Costulas and Ray Randolph, who entered edits into the files; Edie Freedman and Nancy Priest, who designed the cover and interior format, respectively; and Seth Maislin, who developed the index.

Special thanks go to our technical editor, Brian Laskey. Brian went beyond the call of duty not only by identifying problems in the scripts, but also by researching and fixing them. Brian's depth of knowledge and unassuming nature makes him an invaluable resource, as well as a good friend.

A few other individuals who deserve individual mention include the following: Noorali Sonawalla, who created the initial gendb script, used in the crdb script; Ramesh Meda, who created the initial *autoplan.sql* script; Rich Niemiec, whose knowledge of Oracle is surpassed only by his willingness to share it; Buff Emslie, who provided access to her vast technical library and helped introduce the world of Oracle books and publishers; and Larry Ellison, whose product allows us to pursue a career path other than slinging burgers in a fast-food restaurant.

I

Overview

This part of the book contains a single chapter that introduces the scripts we've included on the CD-ROM provided with this book. The chapter explains how to install the scripts in your system and discusses how to use both the scripts and their accompanying documentation. It also contains a cross-reference listing showing all of the scripts provided with this book, along with a brief description of their functions.

1

Introduction

Over the years, the authors have created and assembled a vast collection of Oracle utilities and UNIX shell scripts. We developed these scripts in order to solve day-to-day database reliability and performance analysis problems, as well as to assist in the development and maintenance of Oracle applications. In addition, we created a variety of highly specialized but infrequently-run scripts to detect database and/or operating system problems or to identify other exceptions. We've extensively tested all of these routines, and they've been in production use on a daily basis.

We believe that these scripts and other tools will allow our fellow Oracle database administrators and developers to create and use a comprehensive environment of interoperative tools. We've carefully planned the script architecture so that common scripts are called from higher-level scripts. This isolation of functionality allows DBAs to easily customize the scripts in order to match their companies' specific business rules and/or system configurations.

When you are implementing or modifying any of the scripts, be sure to check for any restrictions or dependencies (e.g., naming conventions, files that must be available). These are listed in the descriptions of the scripts in the following chapters. For your convenience, they are also included as comments at the beginning of the script files themselves.

WARNING   Since no two sites have the identical vendor implementation of Ora-
           cle and the operating system, you *must* test each script you plan to
           use in order to ensure that it runs correctly on your specific hard-
           ware/software platform. While we have invested a considerable
           amount of time and effort in the development of these scripts, it is
           impossible to guarantee that each script will always properly oper-
           ate on every possible platform. All of these scripts have been tested
           and will work on most platforms without any modifications, but it is
           up to you to test them to be sure that they will properly work on a
           particular platform.

           Most of the scripts have been tested on Oracle versions as far back
           as 7.0.16, although some of them require more recent versions of
           Oracle (noted in the detailed descriptions of the scripts). Similarly,
           most of the shell scripts have been tested on HP, IBM, Pyramid, and
           Sun SOLARIS systems.

Converting to Other Operating Systems

The scripts in this book were developed, and are designed to run, in a UNIX operating system environment. However, please do not let that fact deter you from
using the scripts if you are running in another (non-UNIX) environment. One of
the strengths of Oracle has always been its portability, and since the bulk of the
scripts are written in standard Oracle Structured Query Language (SQL), these
scripts are portable as well.

There are two basic types of scripts found in this book (and on the accompanying
CD-ROM):

* *SQL scripts* are well-known to most Oracle DBAs and developers; they are
  written in SQL to run under Oracle's SQL*Plus product, and are normally portable to any operating system in which Oracle runs. These scripts are easily
  identified by the extension "*.sql*" in the script name; in this book, they are
  also identified as SQL scripts by the "File Type" entry at the top of each script
  description.

* *UNIX shell scripts* are UNIX-specific programs that perform a series of commands and functions. The scripts in this book are written to run under the
  Korn or Bourne shells; they are identified as shell scripts by the "File Type"
  entry at the top of each script description.

In this book, many of the shell scripts are used to execute a SQL script in an
orderly manner. In other operating systems, such a script might be called a
"batch" script or file. For example, a shell script might set some environment variables, execute a SQL script, and display the corresponding output on the screen.

In this case, you could execute the SQL script independently, or use the native scripting language of your operating system to write a batch script with similar functionality.

Consider the following shell script, which is used to list all roles in the database and the usernames who have been granted each role (this simplified example has been adapted from the *rolelist* script found in this book):

```
echo "Enter the ORACLE SID of the database to be accessed: \c"
read sid
SID=$mysid
. define
sqlplus -s / @$DBA/rolelist
lp -c rolelist.lis
rm rolelist.lis
```

This script gets the SID of the database from the user (via the keyboard), sets the correct environment (via the *define* script), calls SQL*Plus to execute the *rolelist.sql* script (located in the DBA directory), and finally prints the resulting report and deletes the report file.

You can readily convert this script to another operating system. For example, the following DCL file will perform the same function in a DEC VMS environment (note that in this example SID is a symbol and $DBA is a logical name):

```
$ INQUIRE SID /NOPUNC "Enter the ORACLE SID of the database to be accessed: "
$ @define
$ sqlplus -s /@$DBA:rolelist
$ print rolelist.lis;
$ delete rolelist.lis;
```

Similarly, the following would work in a DOS/Windows environment (note that *accept* is a utility that reads a value from the keyboard and stores it in the indicated environment variable):

```
echo Enter the Oracle SID of the database to be accessed
accept SID
ORA_SID=$SID
sqlplus -s / /DBA/rolelist.sql
copy rolelist.lis lpt1:
del rolelist.lis
```

Or you could simply execute SQL*Plus directly from the keyboard and then print the resulting file:

```
sqlplus -s $DBA/rolelist
print rolelist.lis
del rolelist.lis
```

Of course, some of the shell scripts are more complex, or perform UNIX-specific functions; our point here is that most of the scripts provided are readily transportable to other operating environments.

TIP	For more information about UNIX shell scripts, refer to a good UNIX book; one we recommend is *UNIX in a Nutshell* (O'Reilly & Associates, Second Edition, 1992).

Installing the Scripts

All of the scripts covered in this book are located on the accompanying CD-ROM the book. (See "About the CD-ROM" in the Preface for information about the CD-ROM contents and organization.) Before you can use the scripts, you must copy them from the CD-ROM to your system. As written, the scripts are expected to be installed in two different directories:

$DBA

> This directory contains scripts that are generally useful to the DBA. You should create a directory with the appropriate permissions to hold these scripts. You might want to have this directory owned by the Oracle owner and belong to group DBA. In such a case, a permission of 750 (read, write, execute to the owner, read and execute to the DBA group) might be appropriate. If you do not want to define a DBA group, set the protection to 700, which allows read/write/execute access only to the DBA.

$TOOLS

> This directory contains the rest of the scripts, which are generally useful to both DBAs and developers. Again, create a separate directory. This directory may also be owned by the "oracle" owner, but might belong to group DEV. Permission can be set to 755, which gives all permissions (read/write/execute) to the owner and gives read and execute privilege to both the group and any other users.

Defining Directories

You may select any directory names you choose; just be certain to define the environment variables DBA and TOOLS to point to the desired directory. For example, if you use */usr/scripts/dba* as your DBA directory, and */usr/scripts/tools* as your TOOLS directory, then the following UNIX code will define the correct environment:

```
DBA=/usr/scripts/dba
export DBA
TOOLS=/usr/scripts/tools
export TOOLS
```

The variables $DBA and $TOOLS can be used to refer to these directories.

The scripts on the CD-ROM have been organized according to this basic directory structure. The *DBA* subdirectory contains all files that should be copied to your *$DBA* directory, and the *TOOLS* subdirectory contains all files for the *$TOOLS* directory.

For your convenience, UNIX tar files and zip files have also been included. See "About the CD-ROM" in the Preface for details.

If you will be running the scripts on a UNIX system, the following steps will help you get your scripts installed:

1. Create a directory for DBA scripts.

2. Create a directory for TOOLS scripts.

3. Define the environment variables $DBA and $TOOLS.

4. Copy the file *dba.tar* to *$DBA* (you can mount the CD-ROM on your system, or NFS mount it on another system on your network, or use FTP to transfer the file from a PC workstation).

5. Copy the file *tools.tar* to $TOOLS.

6. Expand the DBA scripts as follows:

   ```
   cd $DBA
   tar -xvf dba.tar
   ```

7. Expand the TOOLS scripts as follows:

   ```
   cd $TOOLS
   tar -xvf tools.tar
   ```

8. Modify the PATH to include the $TOOLS variable defined in 2. above. In the Korn and Bourne shells this can be done by adding the following statement to the user *.profile* script:

   ```
   PATH=$PATH:$TOOLS
   ```

   Although it is not required, you may find it useful to add $DBA to the PATH as well.

Creating the Environment

To create the correct environment for the scripts in this book, you must modify the *$TOOLS/database* script. This script contains a list of all Oracle databases and their corresponding parameters. The file is used by many scripts to verify a user-supplied Oracle SID or to acquire an associated parameter. It is a simple text file that you can edit using any ASCII editor. A sample file is provided, but the file *must* be created with correct values before the scripts in this book will function.

Creating the Username

One restriction common to many of the scripts provided here is the requirement that an OPS$username account must exist. If you do not already have an existing OPS$username account, create one by performing the following steps:

1. Log into the Oracle database as the SYSTEM username.

2. Type the following:

    ```
    CREATE USER OPS$username IDENTIFIED EXTERNALLY;
    ```

    where username matches your current UNIX login name.

3. Type the following:

    ```
    GRANT CONNECT, RESOURCE, DBA TO OPS$username;
    ```

4. Type the following:

    ```
    EXIT
    ```

This will allow the scripts (and yourself) to access Oracle by simply typing,

```
sqlplus /
```

at the UNIX system prompt. No username or password needs to be specified. This avoids the security problem of enclosing usernames and passwords in all of your script files.

Now make the required modifications to the database script, and you are ready to unleash the power of the script collection presented in this book.

Installation Summary

The following is a summary of the steps you must complete before attempting to run the scripts in this book:

1. Create directories for DBA and TOOLS, assign the DBA and TOOLS environment variables to them, and add $TOOLS to the user PATH.

2. Copy the scripts from the CD-ROM into the appropriate directories.

3. Edit the database file to include the appropriate parameters for your Oracle databases.

4. Edit the *fixcase* script if necessary to match your site's standards.

5. Edit the *mailto* script to enable automatic email notifications.

6. Create an OPS$ account with DBA privileges.

7. If you are using the backup scripts, follow the installation and configuration instructions in Chapter 6, *Database Backup Utilities*.

How the Scripts Work

In many cases the scripts contained in this book are actually pairs of scripts. The typical operation of these "paired" scripts follows:

1. A UNIX shell script is executed by entering the script name from the UNIX command line (sometimes with parameters as indicated in the script documentation).

2. The UNIX shell script makes calls to other scripts to initialize the UNIX environment, validate arguments, etc.

3. A SQL script (often with the same name as the shell script, but with an extension of *.sql*) is called. Arguments may be passed to the SQL script, or the SQL script may prompt the user for input (like the name of a table).

4. The SQL script may create an output file, and sometimes one or more temporary Oracle tables.

5. Control will return to the shell script, which will display the output file on the terminal screen.

Since many of the *.sql* scripts create output files (see Appendix C, *SQL Scripts That Create Output Files* and Appendix D, *Output Files Created By SQL Scripts* for cross-references to these files), these files are usually available for further processing. In addition, most scripts that display the file on the terminal screen contain a commented *lp* command that may be uncommented if you desire printed output.

Other scripts create SQL files as their output. These files are designed to be executed by Oracle's SQL*Plus, and of course may be editted just like any other SQL script. For example, the script *crindexs.sql* creates a file called *cr_index.sql*, which contains all of the SQL statements necessary to recreate all indexes in your database. This file can be run at any time using SQL*Plus.

What Can I Do with the Scripts?

Table 1-1 provides a list of tasks that a DBA or developer might want to perform, and the corresponding scripts from this book that will perform those tasks.

NOTE   Only those scripts that perform a particular task are listed here; there are many other scripts included that are considered "support" or "internal" scripts—that is, they are called by one of the "main" scripts to perform a specialized function, but may not be useful by themselves. These scripts have not been included, although they are documented in the book.

Table 1-1. Oracle Script Summary

If You Want To...	Use This Script...	Chapter
Analyze dump and trace files every five minutes	every5	4
Analyze tables and indexes using ANALYZE COMPUTE STATISTICS	analyze.sql	8
Analyze the alert file for errors	alertlog	4
Analyze the appropriateness of indexes without creating statistics	analinds.sql	8
Back up archived log files	backarch	6
Calculate the age of a file in days	days_old	11
Calculate the average row size for a table	avgrow.sql	8
Check a table's columns for special characters (more than ten columns)	chktabl2.sql	8
Check a table's columns for special characters (up to ten columns)	chktable.sql	8
Check create database log for errors	chkcrdb	8
Confirm that a table name is valid and exists	istable	8
Create a file containing statistics and SQL for a single session	sesstats.sql	3
Create a file containing a detailed tablespace analysis	tabanal.sql	8
Create a file containing a list of all database files ordered by directory	locate2.sql	8
Create a file containing a list of all dependencies in the database	depend.sql	8
Create a file containing a list of all indexed columns	indcols.sql	8
Create a file containing a list of all invalid objects	invalid.sql	8
Create a file containing a list of existing locks	locks.sql	4
Create a file containing a list of freespace in the database	free.sql	8
Create a file containing a report of session waits	waitstat.sql	3
Create a file containing alert file errors	alertlog.sql	4
Create a file containing all grants against columns	colgrant.sql	5
Create a file containing all grants to specific user or role	grant_to.sql	5
Create a file containing all profiles in the database	profiles.sql	5
Create a file containing all security privileges for a user	privlist.sql	5
Create a file containing all security privileges for a user	privs.sql	5
Create a file containing all table privileges	alltabp.sql	5
Create a file containing all user account quotas	quotas.sql	5
Create a file containing all user accounts	usrs.sql	5
Create a file containing ANALYZE VALIDATE STRUCTURE commands	validate.sql	4
Create a file containing configuration and sizing information	tblsize.sql	8

Table 1-1. Oracle Script Summary (continued)

If You Want To...	Use This Script...	Chapter
Create a file containing database structures and associated files	file_use.sql	8
Create a file containing grants against an object segregated by type of grant recipient	tabgrant.sql	5
Create a file containing grants on objects	allgrant.sql	5
Create a file containing grants on users and roles	allprivs.sql	5
Create a file containing list of current users	dbousers.sql	2
Create a file containing roles and grantees of those roles	rolelist.sql	5
Create a file containing rollback segment information	rollback.sql	3
Create a file containing statistics for an individual table	tablstat.sql	8
Create a file containing tablespace utilization statistics	tablesp.sql	8
Create a file describing all V$ and DBA_ views	descview.sql	8
Create a file of SQL statements being executed	dbo_sql.sql	8
Create a list of all installed Oracle products	products	8
Create a new index on a table	crindex	8
Create a new OPS$ account	makeops.sql	5
Create a new user with the same properties as an existing user	copyuser	5
Create a report of all object auditing options in effect	auditobj.sql	5
Create a report of all statement and object auditing options in effect	audobj.sql	5
Create a report of all statement auditing options in effect	auditst.sql	5
Create a report of the current month's usage by username	audses.sql	5
Create a report of the most frequently used tables and views	audhot.sql	5
Create a script containing nonunique index drop and create statements	cdindex.sql	8
Create a script to create an OPS$ user account for an existing username	makeops.sql	5
Create a script to grant a user all privileges on non-system objects	grantall.sql	5
Create a script to recreate grants for tables and columns	getgrant.sql	5
Create a SQL script containing INSERT statements for use in tablsize	tblsizec.sql	8
Create a SQL script to create a new index on a table	cindex	8
Create a SQL script to fix ownership of primary keys	fixowner.sql	8
Create a SQL script to list the contents of X$ tables	fixtable.sql	8
Create a SQL script to recreate a control file	ccontrol	6
Create a SQL script to recreate all clusters	crclusts.sql	8

Table 1-1. Oracle Script Summary (continued)

If You Want To...	Use This Script...	Chapter
Create a SQL script to recreate all comments	crcomms.sql	8
Create a SQL script to recreate all constraints on tables	crconstr.sql	8
Create a SQL script to recreate all database links	crlinks.sql	8
Create a SQL script to recreate all functions	crfuncs.sql	8
Create a SQL script to recreate all grants	crgrants.sql	8
Create a SQL script to recreate all indexes	crindexs.sql	8
Create a SQL script to recreate all package bodies	crbodys.sql	8
Create a SQL script to recreate all packages	crpacks.sql	8
Create a SQL script to recreate all procedures	crprocs.sql	8
Create a SQL script to recreate all profiles	crprofs	8
Create a SQL script to recreate all roles	crroles.sql	8
Create a SQL script to recreate all sequences	crseqs.sql	8
Create a SQL script to recreate all snapshot logs	crsnlogs.sql	8
Create a SQL script to recreate all snapshots	crsnaps.sql	8
Create a SQL script to recreate all synonyms	crsyns.sql	8
Create a SQL script to recreate all triggers	crtrigs.sql	8
Create a SQL script to recreate all user accounts	crusers.sql	8
Create a SQL script to recreate all views	crviews.sql	8
Create a SQL script to recreate sized tables and indexes	tblsize.sql	8
Create a SQL script to recreate sized tablespaces	tblsize.sql	8
Create a SQL script to recreate the database structure	crdb	8
Create a SQL script to resize an existing table	resize	8
Create a unique temporary file name	mktemp	11
Create a UNIX script to back up database files	creback	6
Create a UNIX script to restore database files	creback	6
Create all nonunique indexes for a table	cdindex	8
Create all SQL scripts required to drop tables	ddl	8
Create all SQL scripts required to recreate tables	ddl	8
Create an *opcard* for Alexandria Backup	cr_alex	6
Create an OPS$ account	creops	5
Define an RCS environment variable	lib	9
Define parameters for DBA-related scripts	dbabatch	10
Define the characteristics of your database instances	database	2
Define the UNIX environment	define	2
Delete obsolete archived log files	delarch	6
Determine if database is started	isdbo	2

Table 1-1. Oracle Script Summary (continued)

If You Want To...	Use This Script...	Chapter
Determine start/stop status of concurrent manager for applications	is_mgr	7
Determine the status of the database (up or down)	dbo_stat	2
Disable all primary key, unique, and foreign key constraints	discon.sql	8
Display a list of all invalid objects	invalid	8
Display a detailed analysis of a tablespace	tabanal	8
Display a list of all database files ordered by directory	location	8
Display a list of all indexed columns	indcols	8
Display a list of all nondata objects	nondata.sql	8
Display a list of columns in a table	cindexd.sql	8
Display a list of files that were backed up	backdisp	6
Display a list of locked RCS files	reservs	9
Display a report of freespace in the database	free	8
Display all database structures and associated files	file_use	8
Display all dependencies in the database	depend	8
Display all grants against columns	colgrant	5
Display constraints with owner different from table owner	bad_cons.sql	8
Display grants on objects	allgrant	5
Display grants on users and roles	allprivs.sql	5
Display HP/UX memory statistics	allmemry	12
Display processes connected to the database	connect.sql	3
Display rollback segment information	rollback	3
Display statistics for an individual table	tablstat	8
Display the amount of free memory	freemem	12
Display the current status of the concurrent manager	chkcm	7
Display the date and time the instance was started	instance.sql	8
Display the history of a program in RCS	history	9
Display the owner and tablespace for a table	tableown	8
Display the owner and tablespace for a table	tableown.sql	8
Display the plan output from EXPLAIN PLAN	autoplan.sql	9
Drop a specified object	drop_obj	8
Drop all nonunique indexes for a table	cdindex	8
Enable all primary key, unique, and foreign key constraints	enacon.sql	8
Enforce a 10-minute timeout while waiting for database shutdown	dbostopt	2
Export an entire database	xport	8

Table 1-1. Oracle Script Summary (continued)

If You Want To...	Use This Script...	Chapter
Get the name of the operating system	getsyi	11
Grant SELECT on objects to the READONLY role	readonly.sql	5
Grant SELECT on specific tables to users to run scripts	grantool	5
Import an entire database	mport	8
Kill a UNIX process	killunix	10
Kill an Oracle session	dbakill	10
Lock a file in RCS	reserve	9
Make the database available to menus	online	2
Modify the case of a parameter according to local standards	fixcase	2
Perform a backup on a specific database	backPROD	6
Perform a complete backup	backup	6
Perform ANALYZE VALIDATE STRUCTURE on all tables and indexes	validate.sql	4
Perform grants on tables required to run scripts	grantool.sql	5
Provide menu access to databases	menu	2
Remove a database and all associated files	dbdelete	8
Remove old backup files	backcln	6
Remove the database from menus	offline	2
Remove trailing white space from records in a file	trunc	11
Rename a column	renamcol.sql	8
Replace a file in RCS	replace	9
Replace a portion of the UNIX path	replpath	11
Report all existing locks in the database	locks.sql	4
Report all grants to a specific user or role	grant_to	5
Report all profiles in the database	profiles	5
Report all roles and to whom they were granted	rolelist	5
Report all security privileges for a user	privlist	5
Report all security privileges for a user	privs	5
Report all user account quotas	quotas	5
Report all user accounts	usrs	5
Report grants against an object segregated by type of grant recipient	tabgrant	5
Report Oracle and UNIX performance statistics	monitor	3
Show current users of the database	dbousers	2
Shut down the database	dbostop	2
Specify database access by user	menu.dat	2

Table 1-1. Oracle Script Summary (continued)

If You Want To...	Use This Script...	Chapter
Start SQL*Net listeners	startnet	2
Start the concurrent manager	startm	7
Start the database	dbostart	2
Stop SQL*Net listeners	stopnet	2
Stop the concurrent manager	stopm	7
Unlock a previously locked RCS file	unreserv	9
Verify that an SID is valid	valid_db	2
Wait for online redo logs to be archived	archwait	6

Using the Script Descriptions

The following chapters contain detailed descriptions of the scripts that are contained on the CD-ROM. This is the basic documentation for each of the scripts, and is provided to help you understand the functions and operation of the scripts.

We have adopted a standard style for the documentation of each script. Here are samples of two script documentation descriptions:

profiles

Directory: *$DBA*
File Type: Shell Script
Edit Required: No
Output File: Screen
Syntax: `profiles [sid]`

sid

> The optional Oracle SID for the database to be reported. If omitted, all databases will be reported.

This script creates a report of all profiles that are defined in the specified database (or all databases if no database is specified).

profiles.sql

Directory: *$DBA*
File Type: SQL Script
Edit Required: No
Output File: *profiles.lst*

This script is called by the *profiles* script to create the report file.

Sample report

```
PROFILES - Profiles

Profile            Resource
Name               Name                            Limit
---------------    ------------------------        ---------------
DEFAULT            COMPOSITE_LIMIT                 UNLIMITED
DEFAULT            SESSIONS_PER_USER              UNLIMITED
DEFAULT            CPU_PER_SESSION                UNLIMITED
DEFAULT            CPU_PER_CALL                   UNLIMITED
DEFAULT            LOGICAL_READS_PER_SESSION UNLIMITED
DEFAULT            LOGICAL_READS_PER_CALL     UNLIMITED
DEFAULT            IDLE_TIME                      UNLIMITED
DEFAULT            CONNECT_TIME                   UNLIMITED
DEFAULT            PRIVATE_SGA                    UNLIMITED

9 rows selected.
```

The following elements are included in the documentation for each script:

Name

> The name of the script.

Directory

> The directory where the script can be found: either *$DBA* for the directory specified for DBA scripts at installation, or *$TOOLS* for the directory specified for other (non-DBA) files at installation.

File Type

> The type of file. Most scripts are either UNIX shell scripts (denoted by no extension; for example, *profiles* above), or SQL scripts (denoted by an extension of *.sql*; for example, *profiles.sql* above).

Edit Required

> This indicates whether you are required to make changes to this file before running it. Some files may indicate that editing is optional, which means that some changes may be required to conform to standards at your particular installation.

Output File

The name of the output file (if any) produced by this script. "Screen" indicates that output is directed to the terminal screen. Note that screen output may be redirected to a file or other device if desired.

Script Description

A description of what the script does, along with any other information that might be necessary to successfully run the script. For example, if a script prompts for input, we'll note this in the body of the description.

In addition to the elements listed above, the following may be included in the documentation for a particular script, depending on the characteristics of that script:

Syntax

For scripts that require command line parameters, a syntax section is included. The documentation for the *profiles* script above shows that there is an optional (because it is enclosed in brackets) argument *sid* which can be included on the command line. The parameter explanation indicates that this is the Oracle System Identifier (SID) for the database and that if it is omitted, all databases will be reported.

Sample Report/Output

In cases where sample output helps your understanding of the script, it has been included. Not all script documentation pages include sample output, since much of the output produced is obvious and self-explanatory.

II

Scripts for DBAs

The scripts described in this part of the book are aimed primarily at Oracle database administrators (DBAs). They are designed to provide a number of control and monitoring tools required for the day-to-day operation and support of a modern Oracle database. Most of these scripts require DBA privileges, and therefore may not be useful to Oracle developers and designers; certainly, though, both developers and designers (especially those aspiring to become DBAs!) are encouraged to become familiar with this collection of scripts and reports.

2

Database Control Utilities

The scripts described in this chapter allow the DBA to easily start up, shut down, and check the status of the Oracle database or SQL*Net. By having a consistent way to perform these actions, you will gain better control over your operations, and in this way, you'll reduce errors or even eliminate them.

Many of these scripts are also called by other scripts when they need to perform specialized operations on the database. Therefore, the calling scripts must also take into account any site-specific modifications made to these scripts. This modularity provides for a very flexible and easy-to-maintain environment.

database

Directory: *$TOOLS*
File Type: Data File
Edit Required: Yes
Output File: No

This file is referenced by many of the scripts in this book; they access this file to obtain the characteristics of the database being processed. The file contains one line for each database, and each line of the file contains the following information:

1. A tilde (~) to mark the beginning of each line; if you're using the Korn shell, you must skip this tilde only for the first line in this file

2. The Oracle database System Identifier (SID)

3. A colon

4. The name of the Oracle Applications environment file (in $APPL_TOP), if any

5. A colon

6. Username for access to the database via Applications Object Library (AOL), if any

7. A colon

8. The Oracle Applications APPL_TOP value for the database, if any

9. A colon

10. The $ORACLE_BASE value for this database

11. A colon

12. The $ORACLE_HOME value for this database

13. A colon

14. An optional description of this database to appear in the menu (if using a menu script file)

15. A colon (to mark the end of the preceding field)

Here is a sample of the *database* file for two Oracle databases (running different versions of Oracle), not running Oracle Applications:

```
~PROD::::/u01/home/oracle:/u01/home/oracle/product/7.2.3:Production database:
~DEV::::/u02/home/oracle:/u02/home/oracle/product/7.2.3:Development database:
```

This sample of the *database* file is also for a system running two Oracle databases with different versions, and also running Oracle Applications:

```
~PROD:APPLPROD:APPLSYS:/u01/appldev/rel10.5:/u01/home/oracle:
/u01/home/oracle/product/7.3.2:Production database:
~DEV:APPLDEV:APPLSYS:/u02/appldev/rel10.5:/u02/home/oracle:
/u02/home/oracle/product/7.3.2:Development database:
```

This file is a superset of the *oratab* file (automatically created when the Oracle RDBMS is installed). It is usually located in */etc* or */var/opt/oracle*, and is required because other scripts need the additional information for each database in order to perform their functions properly. The *database* file is read by the *define* script.

You must edit the sample *database* file for your site before you use any script that depends on the data contained in this file.

dbo_stat

Directory: *$DBA*
File Type: Shell Script
Edit Required: No
Output File: No

This script determines the current status of the specified database, and exits with a value of 0 if the database is started; otherwise, it returns a status of 1. It is used when a script needs to know whether or not a database has been started. It is executed by the *backup, crearch, dbostop, dbostart,* and *stat* scripts.

dbostart

Directory: *$DBA*

File Type: Shell Script

Edit Required: No

Output File: No

Syntax: dbostart *sid [exclusive]*

sid

> A required parameter that specifies the ORACLE_SID of the database to be started.

exclusive

> An optional parameter. If specified, it causes the database to be started using the STARTUP RESTRICT command; if it is omitted, STARTUP NORMAL is used.

This script is used to start the specified database (in normal or restricted mode). No error is returned if the database has already been started. The *online* script is called if the database is started in normal mode (in order to make the database available through any menu system; see the *menu* script description). If the database does not start within two minutes, an error is returned.

dbostop

Directory: *$DBA*

File Type: Shell Script

Edit Required: No

Output File: No

Syntax: dbostop *sid [shutdown]*

sid

> A required parameter that specifies the ORACLE_SID of the database to be shut down.

shutdown

> An optional parameter; if specified, it may be one of the following case-insensitive values:

> *NOOFFLINE*

>> Prevents the *offline* script from being called. The default is "offline," which makes the database unavilable from a menu.

> *ABORT*

>> Causes the SHUTDOWN ABORT command to be executed. The default is IMMEDIATE, which causes the SHUTDOWN IMMEDIATE command to be executed to shut down the database.

This script shuts down (normal or abort) the specified database. No error is returned if the database is already shut down. Any concurrent manager for the database must have already been shut down before running this script. The *offline* script is called in order to remove the database from any menu system (see the *menu* script description), unless prohibited by a command line option. The script includes a workaround for any Oracle "space leak" problem.

If the database is being shut down with the SHUTDOWN IMMEDIATE clause (the default option), the *dbostop* script will wait up to ten minutes for the shutdown to complete. If the database has not shut down within ten minutes, it will terminate the current *dbostop* script and will then reexecute the *dbostop* script using the SHUTDOWN ABORT clause. If the database still does not shut down within two minutes, an error is returned.

Restrictions

- This script must operate under the Korn shell in order to support a background job.

- The *define, fixcase, mktemp, is_dbo, mailto, offline,* and *valid_db* scripts must exist and be found in the PATH.

- The PS_OPTS environment variable must be defined (this is usually done by the *$HOME/dbabatch* script).

- Additional restrictions listed for the *define* script (which is called by *dbostop*) must be observed; see the description of *define*.

WARNING   Any script calling *dbostop* must include a "wait" command to ensure that all background processes have been completed before continuing.

---

dbostopt

Directory: *$DBA*
File Type: Shell Script
Edit Required: No
Output File: No

This script is used to implement a 10-minute timeout for the *dbostop* script. See the *dbostop* description for details.

dbousers

Directory: *$TOOLS*
File Type: Shell Script
Edit Required: No
Output File: *dbousers.lst*
Syntax: dbousers *[sid]*

sid

> The Oracle System Identifier for the database; if omitted, all databases listed in the *database* file will be used.

This script displays a report of all of the current users of one or more databases. It displays the contents of any *$TOOLS/dbousers.inf* file (so that any other database-specific information can be included in the report). It executes *dbousers.sql* for the designated database(s).

See the comments within this script for instructions on how to allow non-DBA users to execute the script to obtain the report.

Each line of the report will show the following information for each of the logged-in users:

> Oracle username
> Operating system username
> Oracle session ID
> Session status
> Session type
> Operating system process ID
> Operating system terminal name
> Whether or not this session is waiting on a lock
> The type of SQL command that is being executed

Sample report

```
10/27/97                    DBOUSERS - Database Users for DEV


        Oracle          O/S                        O/S              Lock
        Username        UsernameSid Stat  Type     Pid     Term     Wait  Command
        ------------    ---------------------------  ------  -------------- --------
        OPS$ORACLE      oracle   7  Act   User     17887   pts/0
                        oracle   1  Act   Back     16988   ?
                        oracle   2  Act   Back     16990   ?
                        oracle   3  Act   Back     16992   ?
```

```
oracle   4   Act   Back   16994    ?
oracle   5   Act   Back   16996    ?
```

6 rows selected.

In this report, since only one person was logged onto the database, only one user is displayed.

dbousers.sql

Directory: *$DBA*
File Type: SQL Script
Edit Required: No
Output File: *dbousers.lst*

This script is called by the *dbousers* script to create the desired report, as described in the previous section.

define

Directory: *$TOOLS*
File Type: Shell Script
Edit Required: Yes
Output File: No

This script is used to define database-specific information for a given database (specified in the ORACLE_SID environment variable). The following environment variables are set by this script:

ADMIN
    Contains the *$ORACLE_BASE/admin/$ORACLE_SID* directory.

APPL_TOP
    Contains the $APPL_TOP definition (if Oracle Applications are installed).

ENVNAME
    Contains the name of the Oracle Applications environment file (if Oracle applications are installed)

ORACLE_BASE
    Contains the $ORACLE_BASE definition.

ORACLE_HOME
    Contains the $ORACLE_HOME definition.

ORACLE_SID
    Contains the $ORACLE_SID definition.

USRNAME

Contains the username to use when executing Applcations Object Library (AOL) calls (if Oracle Applications are installed).

In addition, the *define* script does the following:

- Executes the appropriate Oracle Applications environment file for the specified database (if Oracle Applications are installed).

- Defines the PS_OPTS environment variable that contains the UNIX-specific *ps* options.

This script is basically a superset of the Oracle-supplied *oraenv* file, and is used because additional information needs to be provided to the other scripts so they can perform their functions properly. The *oraenv* file is automatically created when the Oracle RDBMS is installed, and is usually located in */opt/bin* or */usr/local/bin*. The *define* script gets its data by reading the *$TOOLS/database* file, and calls the *getsyi* and *replpath* scripts. If Oracle Applications are being used, $APPL_TOP/$ENVNAME.env must also exist.

This script is executed by almost every other script in this book to ensure that the proper environment is created.

fixcase

Directory: *$TOOLS*
File Type: Shell Script
Edit Required: Optional
Output File: No
Syntax: `fixcase sid`

sid

The Oracle SID for the database; the specification will be converted into the appropriate case.

This script allows the implementation of site-specific rules regarding the case of an Oracle SID. When it is executed with the user-supplied Oracle SID as its only parameter, it returns the same Oracle SID in the required case (uppercase or lowercase). This script is used in most scripts that accept user input, so that the correct Oracle SID will be returned, even if the user enters it in the wrong case.

As distributed, *fixcase* will automatically convert the Oracle SID that is passed to it into lowercase, but it may be modified to enforce a site's particular SID naming convention.

is_dbo

Directory: *$TOOLS*
File Type: Shell Script
Edit Required: No
Output File: No

This script is called by other scripts in order to determine the status of the specified database. It returns an exit status of 0 if the specified database is down, or 1 if the database has been started. It determines the status of the database by checking the operating system processes for a *pmon* process for the given database. It also determines whether the database has crashed (In this case there will be no pmon process, but an *sgadef<SID>.dbf* file will still exist in the *$ORACLE_HOME/ dbs* directory.)

menu

Directory: *$DBA*
File Type: Shell Script
Edit Required: Yes
Output File: No

This is a sample shell script that demonstrates the use of a menu to control access to one or more Oracle databases. Note in particular the use of the *offline* script to determine whether a particular database is available.

NOTE   As provided, this script is very specific to a particular installation, and will probably require significant modification for use at *your* site. It is intended as an example of how a menu system may be written and not as a functional program.

---

menu.dat

Directory: *$TOOLS*
File Type: Data File
Edit Required: Yes
Output File: No

This file is referenced by a menu script to control database access to specific users. Note that this script provides an example of how such an access list might be implemented in an actual menu script, and it must be modified for actual use. The file contains one line for each database user in the following form:

1. The username

2. A colon

3. The names of one or more databases to which this user is to be given access, separated by commas

For example, consider the following *menu.dat* file:

```
lomasky:PROD,STAG,DEV,TEST,DEVSQL
kreines:PROD,TEST
```

User lomasky has access to five databases, while user kreines has access only to PROD and TEST, and has no access to STAG, DEV, or DEVSQL.

offline

Directory: *$DBA*
File Type: Shell Script
Edit Required: No
Output File: No
Syntax: offline *[sid]*

sid
   The Oracle SID of the database to be marked "offline."

When the *offline* script is executed and passed one argument, it "marks" the database as "offline" (removing it from all menus). This script can be used to ensure that users (or any other cooperating scripts) do not try to access a database that has been marked "offline" (such as when the database is being backed up, maintenance is being performed, or some other problem causes the database to be unavailable). It indicates the "offline" status by creating a *$TOOLS/offline.<sid>* file.

This script is executed by the *dbostop* script.

When the *offline* script is executed without any argument, it displays an error message (indicating that the usual argument was omitted); it then displays a list of all of the database SIDs that are currently marked as "offline."

online

Directory: *$DBA*
File Type: Shell Script
Edit Required: No
Output File: No
Syntax: `online [sid]`

sid
>   The Oracle SID of the database to be marked "online."

When the online script is executed and passed one argument, it removes the "offline" status for the specified database (making the database available for display on menus, if a menu script is being used). This action is the exact opposite of the *offline* script. It also makes the database "online" by deleting the *$TOOLS/ offline.<sid>* file.

This script is executed by the *dbostart* script (if the database is not started in exclusive mode).

When the *online* script is executed without any argument, it displays an error message (indicating that the usual argument was omitted), and then displays a list of all of the database SIDs that are currently marked as being "online." (All databases that are not marked as being "offline" are considered to be "online.")

startnet

Directory: *$DBA*
File Type: Shell Script
Edit Required: Yes
Output File: No

This script is used to start the SQL*Net (V2 and/or V1) listeners (typically, after the nightly database backup has been completed). The script uses the executables based upon a specific version of the RDBMS (currently PROD in the script supplied with this book); you will need to edit this file to define the Oracle SID of your site-specific executables that you want to execute.

This script is executed by the *$DBA/back<sid>* and *$DBA/dbo_reopen* scripts. It can also be executed by the appropriate system startup script (for example, */etc/ rc2.d/S99dbora*) to start the SQL*Net listener(s) at system boot time.

stopnet

Directory: *$DBA*
File Type: Shell Script
Edit Required: Yes
Output File: No

This script is used to shut down the SQL*Net (V2 and/or V1) listeners (typically, before the nightly database backup has started). The script uses the executables based upon a specific version of the RDBMS (currently PROD in the script supplied with this book); you will need to edit this file to define the Oracle SID of your site-specific executables that you want to execute. It is executed by the desired *$DBA/back<sid>* and *$DBA/dbo_reopen* scripts.

valid_db

Directory: *$TOOLS*
File Type: Shell Script
Edit Required: No
Output File: No

This script is used to verify that a valid Oracle SID has been specified. It does this by comparing the specified argument against the list of Oracle SID(s) in the *$TOOLS/database* file. If the argument matches any of the Oracle SID(s), an exit status of 0 will be returned; otherwise, an exit status of 2 will be returned.

The *valid_db* script is executed by many of the other scripts described in this book.

3

Database Performance and Trend Analysis Utilities

The scripts in this chapter can be used to analyze the performance of the currently executing SQL statements, report on rollback statement and wait statistics, and display overall Oracle database tuning metrics. UNIX system performance is measured by a that takes a snapshot of the current system's performance metrics.

Poor performance can occur within the Oracle database or within the UNIX operating system. The scripts in this section allow the DBA to view and report on some of the possible situations that can adversely affect database performance.

connect.sql

Directory: *$DBA*
File Type: SQL Script
Edit Required: No
Output File: Screen

This script displays the following information for all of the current database sessions:

- The Oracle process ID
- The operating system PID
- The Oracle session ID
- The Oracle username
- The operating system username

- The time when the user logged on to the database (i.e., connect time)
- The time when the user last performed any activity (i.e., non-idle time)

This script is useful when the DBA needs to view the processes connected to a database, the length of time that they have been connected, and when they last performed any work.

Restrictions

- This script requires that RESOURCE_LIMIT = TRUE be specified in the *INIT.ORA* file.
- As provided, the script will work with Oracle7.3 and above. To use it with Oracle7.2 or below, see the commented portion of the script.

Sample report

```
PID SPID    SID ORA_USER   UNIX_USER  WHEN USER LOGGED ON   WHEN LAST ACTIVITY
---- -----  ----- ---------- ---------- -------------------- --------------------

   7 17742    7 ops$oracle oracle     10/30/97 21:24:36    10/30/97 21:24:36
   9 17812    9 scott      francis    10/30/97 20:43:34    10/30/97 21:26:07
```

monitor

Directory: *$DBA*
File Type: Shell Script
Edit Required: No
Output File: *monitor.lis*

This script creates a report (*monitor.lis*) containing the current UNIX and Oracle database performance monitoring statistics for a specific database. This report will be most useful when you are trying to diagnose a system slowdown in real time, since it allows the DBA to quickly identify any resource shortage(s) by taking a current limited snapshot of the system.

The UNIX statistics displayed vary by operating system. For Sun SOLARIS, the following items of data are displayed:

- Swapping statistics
- CPU job run queue
- Memory paging statistics
- Memory shortfall statistics
- Free memory
- CPU mode percentages

- Disk I/O queue depths
- UNIX read and write cache hit ratios

For HP-UX, the following items of data are displayed:

- Memory paging statistics
- Memory shortfall statistics
- Free memory
- CPU mode percentages
- Disk I/O queue depths

The *monitor.sql* script is executed to retrieve the Oracle database performance statistics for the database specified in the ORACLE_SID environment variable. Since an Oracle slowdown is typically due to inefficient SQL statements, the script displays information regarding the SQL statements that are using the most physical disk I/O and the most logical I/O. Excessive logical I/O can cause often-used data to be pushed out of memory. Excessive physical I/Os usually indicate that full table scans are being performed.

Restrictions

- The *getsyi* and *monitor.sql* scripts are executed to gather the required information. These must exist, and *getsyi* must be found in the PATH.
- An OPS$username account must be created in the current database for the username who is running this script.
- For HP-UX systems, the *free_memory* script must exist and be found in the PATH.
- Currently, only Sun SOLARIS and HP-UX systems are supported for UNIX performance statistics.

Sample report

```
-- Performance Monitoring Report for node syst01 at 10/27/97 08:38:16 --


Collecting UNIX system performance statistics - Please wait 5 seconds...


                Free swap space    1440848

                   Free memory        7648
                CPU user mode           0
              CPU system mode           0
                CPU idle mode          99
```

Analyzing disk system performance statistics - Please wait 10 seconds...

    (The disk subsystem is performing normally...)

Processing UNIX cache performance statistics - Please wait 5 seconds...

Retrieving Oracle database performance statistics - Please wait...

Analyzing performance of database DEV on 10/27/97

Memory pigs - Top 5 queries using the largest amount of logical reads

```
    Buffer
     Gets Username    SID SQL Text
---------- ------------ ------ --------------------------------------------------
   137741 OPS$ORACLE       SELECT 'Column' lvl, c.privilege, c.grantable, c
                           .owner, c.table_name FROM dba_col_privs c UNION
                           SELECT 'Role' Gr_Type, r.granted_role obj, r.adm
                           in_option a, NULL, NULL FROM dba_role_privs r UN
                           ION SELECT 'Sys Priv', s.privilege, s.admin_opti
                           on, NULL, NULL FROM dba_sys_privs s UNION SELECT
                           'Table', t.privilege, t.grantable, t.owner, t.t
                           able_name FROM dba_tab_privs t ORDER BY 1, 2, 3,
                           4, 5

   125485 OPS$ORACLE       select o.name dname, d_timestamp, o2.name pname,
                           p_timestamp from sys.dependency$ d, sys.obj$ o,
                           sys.obj$ o2 where d_obj# = o.obj# and p_obj# =
                           o2.obj#

   110275 OPS$ORACLE       SELECT 'Role' lvl, t.owner, t.table_name, t.gran
                           tee, t.privilege FROM dba_tab_privs t WHERE t.gr
                           antee IN (SELECT role FROM dba_roles WHERE role
                           = t.grantee) UNION SELECT 'User' lvl, t.owner, t
                           .table_name, t.grantee, t.privilege FROM dba_tab
                           _privs t WHERE t.grantee IN (SELECT username FRO
                           M dba_users WHERE username = t.grantee) UNION SE
                           LECT 'Pub' lvl, t.owner, t.table_name, t.grantee
                           , t.privilege FROM dba_tab_privs t WHERE t.grant
                           ee = 'PUBLIC' ORDER BY 1, 2, 3

    54346 OPS$ORACLE       select grantor, grantee, table_name, privilege,
                           decode(owner,grantor,'',owner) Owner, decode(gra
                           ntable,'NO','',grantable) Grantable from dba_tab
                           _privs order by grantor, grantee, table_name

    43533 SYS             select distinct owner from dba_tables
```

monitor.sql

Directory: *$DBA*
File Type: SQL Script
Edit Required: No
Output File: None

This script creates a temporary table in the database and populates it with database statistics for use in the *monitor* script. This is an internal support script and is not normally called directly.

rollback

Directory: *$DBA*
File Type: Shell Script
Edit Required: No
Output File: Screen

This shell script displays a formatted report, containing all of the important rollback statistics for the specified database, in a single concise report. It executes the *rollback.sql* script in order to create the report.

The report includes the following summary information for all rollback segments:

- Number of gets on the rollback segment header

- Number of waits on the rollback segment header

- Ratio of the number of waits to gets on the rollback segment header

For each rollback segment, the following items are included in the report:

- Rollback segment name

- Number of header waits for the rollback segment header; if non-zero, then a transaction had to wait before acquiring a lock in the header of a rollback segment

- Percentage of waits to gets

- Number of header gets (i.e., transactions) on the rollback segment header

- Cumulative number of bytes written to the rollback segment

- Size of the rollback segment, in bytes

- Optimal rollback segment size

- High water mark, in megabytes

- Number of times the rollback segment shrank, eliminating one or more additional extents each time (because it was larger than the optimal size)

- Number of times the rollback segment extended to have a new extent
- Current average size of the active extents, where "active" extents have uncommitted transaction data
- Number of extents
- Average number of active transactions in the rollback segment
- Number of times the rollback segment wrapped from one extent to another
- Total size of freed extents divided by number of shrinks

For each rollback segment which is not "online," the following information is also displayed:

- Rollback segment name
- Tablespace name containing the rollback segment
- Rollback segment status

The report includes additional information on how to properly tune the rollback segments for their optimal size. Rollback segment contention information is also included, so that bottlenecks can be diagnosed and corrected.

Sample report

```
GETS  - # of gets on the rollback segment header: 931
WAITS - # of waits for the rollback segment header: 0
The ratio of Rollback waits/gets is 0%
    If ratio is more than 1%, create more rollback segments
```

Roll Segm Name	Wait	% Wait	Gets	Write	Mb	Opt Mb	Hi Wtr Mb	# Shr ink	# Ext end	Avgsz Activ	# Ext	# Trn	Wr aps	Av Shr
SYSTEM	0	0	142	1768	0		0	0	0	0	4	0	0	0
BRBS	0	0	179	36 k	10	10	10	0	0	0	10	0	0	0
R03	0	0	148	17 k	2	2	2	0	0	0	5	0	0	0
R04	0	0	164	16 k	2	2	2	0	0	0	5	0	0	0
R02	0	0	141	7217	2	2	2	0	0	0	5	0	0	0
R01	0	0	169	18 k	2	2	2	0	0	51 k	5	0	1	0

```
If # Shrink is low:
    If AvShr is low:
        If Avgsz Activ is much smaller than Opt Mb:
            Reduce OPTIMAL (since not many shrinks occur).
    If AvShr is high:
        Good value for OPTIMAL.
If # Shrink is high:
    If AvShr is low:
        Too many shrinks being performed, since OPTIMAL is
        somewhat (but not hugely) too small.
```

```
If AvShr is high:
     Increase OPTIMAL until # of Shrnk decreases.  Periodic
     long transactions are probably causing this.
```

A high value in the #Ext column indicates dynamic extension, in which case you should consider increasing your rollback segment size. (Also, increase it if you get a "Shapshot too old" error).

A high value in the # Extend and # Shrink columns indicate allocation and deallocation of extents, due to rollback segments with a smaller optimal size. It also may be due to a batch processing transaction assigned to a smaller rollback segment. Consider increasing OPTIMAL.

```
Rollback contention for system undo header = 0%    (Total requests = 0)
Rollback contention for system undo block  = 0%    (Total requests = 0)
Rollback contention for undo header        = 0%    (Total requests = 0)
Rollback contention for undo block         = 0%    (Total requests = 0)
If percentage is more than 1%, create more rollback segments
```

rollback.sql

Directory: *$DBA*
File Type: SQL Script
Edit Required: No
Output File: *rollback.lis*

This script is called by the r*ollback* script, and creates a file containing information on rollback segments in the database.

sesstats.sql

Directory: *$DBA*
File Type: SQL Script
Edit Required: No
Output File: *sesstats.lis*

This script creates a report containing the statistics and the SQL statement being executed by a specific session ID in the current database. Before running this script, be sure that the required view and synonym have been created by running *$DBA/dbosqli.sql*. See the "Restrictions" section under the *dbo_sql* script for more information.

The script will prompt for the session ID number, and will then display all of the non-zero Oracle statistics, as well as the current SQL text (if any) for that Oracle session ID.

Sample report

02/27/98   SESSTATS - Statistics for database DEV SID 7

```
USERNAME   Statistic name                                    Value
---------- -------------------------------------------- ----------
OPS$ORACLE CPU used by this session                              1
OPS$ORACLE CPU used when call started                            1
OPS$ORACLE SQL*Net roundtrips to/from client                    47
OPS$ORACLE bytes received via SQL*Net from client             3852
OPS$ORACLE bytes sent via SQL*Net to client                   2083
OPS$ORACLE calls to get snapshot scn: kcmgss                    12
OPS$ORACLE calls to kcmgas                                       1
OPS$ORACLE calls to kcmgrs                                      14
OPS$ORACLE commit cleanout number successfully completed         1
OPS$ORACLE consistent gets                                      29
OPS$ORACLE cursor authentications                               12
OPS$ORACLE db block changes                                      4
OPS$ORACLE db block gets                                        12
OPS$ORACLE deferred (CURRENT) block cleanout applications        1
OPS$ORACLE enqueue releases                                      3
OPS$ORACLE enqueue requests                                      3
OPS$ORACLE execute count                                        17
OPS$ORACLE free buffer requested                                 3
OPS$ORACLE logons cumulative                                     1
OPS$ORACLE logons current                                        1
OPS$ORACLE messages sent                                         1
OPS$ORACLE no work - consistent read gets                       16
OPS$ORACLE opened cursors cumulative                            11
OPS$ORACLE opened cursors current                                1
OPS$ORACLE parse count                                          17
OPS$ORACLE physical reads                                        3
OPS$ORACLE process last non-idle time                    315650474
OPS$ORACLE recursive calls                                      27
OPS$ORACLE redo entries                                          2
OPS$ORACLE redo size                                           490
OPS$ORACLE redo small copies                                     2
OPS$ORACLE redo synch writes                                     1
OPS$ORACLE session connect time                          315650474
OPS$ORACLE session logical reads                                38
OPS$ORACLE session pga memory                                77900
OPS$ORACLE session pga memory max                            77900
OPS$ORACLE session uga memory                                22760
OPS$ORACLE session uga memory max                            22760
OPS$ORACLE table fetch by rowid                                  3
OPS$ORACLE table scan blocks gotten                              2
OPS$ORACLE table scan rows gotten                                2
OPS$ORACLE table scans (short tables)                            4
OPS$ORACLE total number commit cleanout calls                    1
OPS$ORACLE user calls                                           42

44 rows selected.
```

```
10/27/97          SESSTATS - Statistics for database DEV SID 7

SQL Text
---------------------------------------------------------------
select sql_text from dbo_sql_text where sid = 7 order by piece
```

waitstat.sql

Directory: *$DBA*
File Type: SQL Script
Edit Required: No
Output File: *waitstat.lst*

This script creates a report of all session waits in the database for one or all Oracle session IDs in the current database. This information may then be used to determine what events (if any) a process is waiting for in the database. The report also displays the total and average amount of wait time for each event. Events that might indicate a resource contention are flagged with an asterisk (*). In addition, system-wide latch wait events are also displayed.

One parameter is required for this script: the session ID for which you want to print a report (0 means print a report for all sessions).

Sample report

```
Database: DEV              Session and Event Wait Statistics          02/27/98

              ========== SID:  1    Username: PMON ==========

                                  Total       Total        Time       Avg
    Event                         Waits      Timeouts      Waited      Wait
    ------------------------    -----------  -----------  ----------- -----------
    pmon timer                     10406       10406        31323         3*
        Seq#: 10407 Wait Time: Curr duration 300

              ========== SID:  2    Username: DBWR ==========

                                  Total       Total        Time       Avg
    Event                         Waits      Timeouts      Waited      Wait
    ------------------------    -----------  -----------  ----------- -----------
    control file sequential read     122          0            0          0
    db file parallel write           116          0            1          0 *
    db file sequential read           18          0            0          0
    log file sync                     13          0            0          0
    rdbms ipc message              11368       10405        31323          3*

      Seq#: 11638 Wait Time: Curr timeout 224
```

========== SID: 3   Username: LGWR ==========

Event	Total Waits	Total Timeouts	Time Waited	Avg Wait
control file parallel write	63	0	0	0*
control file sequential read	61	0	0	0
db file sequential read	36	0	0	0*
db file single write	36	0	0	0*
log file parallel write	125	0	0	0*
log file sequential read	5	0	0	0*
log file single write	6	0	0	0*
rdbms ipc message	10521	10404	31323	3*

========== SID: 4   Username: SMON ==========

Event	Total Waits	Total Timeouts	Time Waited	Avg Wait
db file scattered read	514	0	2	0*
db file sequential read	289	0	3	0*
smon timer	107	104	31205	292*

  Seq#: 911 Wait Time: Curr sleep time 300 failed 0

========== SID: 5   Username: RECO ==========

Event	Total Waits	Total Timeouts	Time Waited	Avg Wait
db file sequential read	5	0	0	0*
rdbms ipc message	19	19	30663	1614*

  Seq#: 25 Wait Time: Curr timeout 180000

========== SID: 7   Username: OPS$ORACLE ==========

Event	Total Waits	Total Timeouts	Time Waited	Avg Wait
SQL*Net message from client	46	0	0	0*
SQL*Net message to client	46	0	0	0
SQL*Net more data from client	1	0	0	0
control file sequential read	2	0	0	0
Seq#: 142 Wait Time: Curr file# 0 block# 3 blocks 1				
db file sequential read	43	0	0	0*
log file sync	4	0	0	0*

============ SYSTEM-WIDE EVENT STATISTICS ============

Event	Total Waits	Total Timeouts	Time Waited	Avg Wait
rdbms ipc message	21911	20828	9331152	426
pmon timer	10406	10406	3132291	301
db file sequential read	7732	0	1000	0
SQL*Net message to client	5300	0	2	0
SQL*Net message from client	5300	0	60983	12
db file scattered read	668	0	215	0
control file sequential read	559	0	10	0
log file parallel write	127	0	42	0
db file parallel write	116	0	79	1
smon timer	107	104	3120472	29163
control file parallel write	64	0	34	1
log file sync	48	0	15	0
db file single write	36	0	10	0
SQL*Net break/reset to client	31	0	0	0
rdbms ipc reply	10	0	64	6
log file single write	6	0	2	0
log file sequential read	5	0	1	0
SQL*Net more data from client	4	0	0	0
SQL*Net more data to client	3	0	0	0
process startup	1	0	3	3
log file switch completion	1	0	8	8
instance state change	1	0	3	3
write complete waits	1	0	0	0

4

Database Reliability Monitoring Utilities

The DBA needs to be vigilant about monitoring for all of the possible circumstances that can cause the database to halt or fail. These are the most common failures:

- A tablespace runs out of contiguous free space to contain an object that tries to increase in size.

- An object tries to increase its number of extents beyond the maximum allowed for the object.

Other errors usually show up in the alert log file and trace dump files that are created by Oracle.

Hardware (usually disk media) failures can also halt a database. You must know where every file associated with a database is located.

Finally, poorly written application code can lock database objects for exclusive access for a prolonged period. This can cause other applications that need access to the locked objects to halt until the original lock is removed.

The scripts in this chapter will help you analyze the alert log for redo log statistics and errors, monitor the database for any trace dump files that are created, display comprehensive locking information, search for and report on core dump files, and validate the structure of the database tables and indexes.

alertlog

Directory: *$DBA*
File Type: Shell Script
Edit Required: No
Output File: Screen

This script analyzes the Oracle *alert<SID>.log* file for redo log statistics and errors. It creates a report describing the statistics and any errors that it finds. The *alertlog.sql* script is executed by this script in order to create the report.

Restrictions

* The ORACLE_SID and ORACLE_HOME environment variables must be set before running this script.
* An OPS$username account must exist.
* The UTL_FILE_DIR parameter must have been set in the *INIT.ORA* file.

Sample report

```
Analysis of /u01/home/oracle/admin/ddw/bdump/alert_ddw.log on syst01
```

Hourly Bucket	Number of Log Switches	Checkpoint Not Complete	Wait Time (seconds)	Pct Wait per Bucket
05/06/97 08:00:00	7			
05/06/97 17:00:00	3			
05/06/97 18:00:00	5			
05/07/97 09:00:00	19			
05/07/97 10:00:00	7			
05/07/97 12:00:00	11			
05/07/97 17:00:00	9			
05/07/97 18:00:00	39			
05/07/97 19:00:00	19			
05/08/97 08:00:00	35	2	51	1%
05/08/97 09:00:00	46			
05/08/97 10:00:00	48			
05/08/97 11:00:00	20	1	28	1%
05/08/97 12:00:00	5			
05/08/97 13:00:00	33			
05/08/97 14:00:00	46			
05/08/97 15:00:00	30	1	41	1%
05/08/97 16:00:00	15	2	12	0%
05/08/97 17:00:00	72	25	414	12%
05/08/97 18:00:00	61	22	636	18%
05/08/97 19:00:00	63	24	973	27%
05/08/97 20:00:00	58	22	1098	31%
05/08/97 21:00:00	67	22	874	24%
05/08/97 22:00:00	41	20	1492	41%

05/08/97 23:00:00	41	5	41	1%
05/09/97 11:00:00	2			
05/09/97 14:00:00	1			
05/09/97 17:00:00	36			
05/09/97 18:00:00	22			
05/12/97 08:00:00	1			
05/12/97 09:00:00	3			
05/12/97 10:00:00	4			
05/12/97 11:00:00	50	10	107	3%
05/12/97 12:00:00	72	29	873	24%
05/12/97 13:00:00	49	18	884	25%
05/12/97 14:00:00	67	25	1068	30%
05/12/97 15:00:00	45	22	1590	44%
05/12/97 16:00:00	11			
05/12/97 17:00:00	37	6	52	1%
05/13/97 13:00:00	1			
05/13/97 17:00:00	38			
05/13/97 18:00:00	26			
05/13/97 21:00:00	23			
05/13/97 22:00:00	26	6	79	2%
05/14/97 09:00:00	1			
05/14/97 14:00:00	1			
05/14/97 16:00:00	5			
05/14/97 17:00:00	1			
05/14/97 20:00:00	21			
05/14/97 21:00:00	28			
05/14/97 22:00:00	9			
05/15/97 02:00:00	25			
05/15/97 03:00:00	26	6	86	2%
05/15/97 12:00:00	4	1	21	1%
05/16/97 07:00:00	1			
05/16/97 09:00:00	5			
05/16/97 10:00:00	1			
05/16/97 11:00:00	1			
05/16/97 12:00:00	3			
05/16/97 14:00:00	1			
05/16/97 15:00:00	4			
05/16/97 17:00:00	6	1	22	1%
05/16/97 18:00:00	1			
05/17/97 07:00:00	1			
05/17/97 09:00:00	9			
05/17/97 21:00:00	4			
05/18/97 06:00:00	9			
05/18/97 09:00:00	10			
05/18/97 10:00:00	40	6	95	3%
05/18/97 17:00:00	1			
05/18/97 18:00:00	4	1	10	0%
05/18/97 21:00:00	2			
05/19/97 13:00:00	3			
05/19/97 14:00:00	1			
05/19/97 15:00:00	3	1	199	6%
05/19/97 16:00:00	1			
05/19/97 19:00:00	4			
05/19/97 22:00:00	1			

```
05/19/97 23:00:00          37          4          75          2%
05/20/97 00:00:00          13          3          48          1%
05/20/97 15:00:00           1
05/20/97 16:00:00           5
05/20/97 19:00:00          41          7          97          3%
05/21/97 10:00:00           5
05/21/97 14:00:00           4
05/21/97 15:00:00           1
05/21/97 16:00:00           3
05/21/97 18:00:00           1
05/22/97 09:00:00           4          1          34          1%
05/22/97 11:00:00           2
05/22/97 15:00:00           4
05/22/97 18:00:00           3
05/27/97 11:00:00           1
05/27/97 12:00:00           1
```

alertlog.sql

Directory: *$DBA*
File Type: SQL Script
Edit Required: No
Output File: Screen

This script is executed by the *alertlog* script to create its report, as described in the previous section. Note that this script assumes that the *INIT.ORA* parameter UTL_FILE_DIR has been defined.

every5

Directory: *$DBA*
File Type: Shell Script
Edit Required: No
Output File: Screen

This script will automatically check Oracle alert, trace, and dump files for significant errors.

Oracle DBAs are trained to check the database alert log files periodically for errors. The background and user dump file destination directories also need to be checked for expected and unexpected trace dump files. These operations need to be performed for all Oracle databases on every system. Here is a quick quiz:

Q: How frequently do you check for trace dump files in each of your databases?

    a. Never ("I'm too busy")

    b. Never ("I forget")

    c. Only when database availability is affected

d. Only when a filesystem is filled to 100% capacity with trace dump files

e. Frquently, except when I'm sick, on vacation, at IOUG-Alive, etc.

As you can imagine, most DBAs skip this very important function. But monitoring trace dump file activity is essential for the proper operation of the databases. Why?

- Because the alert log file keeps growing every day, eventually filling up the filesystem (and halting the database).

- Because the DBA needs to know *immediately* whenever a database error (such as an ORA-600) or any other unusual condition occurs.

However, the DBA does *not* need to know whenever *any* trace dump file is created, since developers and users create trace dump files by using the SQL Trace facility. These are not problems for the DBA, although if left unchecked, they can eventually fill up the filesystem on which the dump directories are located. Some normal day-to-day operations (such as database shutdown) can also create trace dump files.

Waiting for users to contact you when they cannot access a database is *not* a proactive solution! Most DBAs would like to be able to detect potential database problems *before* they affect the user's accessibility to the database. The *every5* script provides an automatic process that will check every five minutes for the existence of any new trace dump file. For each trace dump file it finds, the script will do the following:

- Analyze its contents
- Filter out "expected" dump files according to a specified set of rules

Detailed comments in the script file explain each of the filters. Depending on the result of the filtering process, the process will perform one of the following actions:

- Delete the trace dump file
- Rename the trace dump file to *.old* (automatically deleting it once it is 15 days old)

- Rename the trace dump file to *.ttt* (automatically deleting it once it is three days old)

- Mail a descriptive message to the DBA

Here are some examples of "expected" trace dump files:

- A user has invoked the SQL Trace operation (such as executing the SQL command, ALTER SESSION SET SQL_TRACE TRUE).

- A PL/SQL routine, which aborts with a runtime error, can create a trace dump file with an ORA-600 error having an argument of 17285.

- A user, which cancels an operation (by pressing the Control/C key), can create an ORA-1013 trace dump file.

- A process, which has aborted because the database has been shut down with the ABORT clause, can create an ORA-1092 trace dump file.

- A "space leak" error creates a trace dump file. The Oracle workaround is to perform a SHUTDOWN ABORT, a STARTUP RESTRICT, and then a SHUTDOWN NORMAL (detected and corrected by using the *dbostop* script to perform database shutdowns), so the trace dump file can always be deleted.

The script will flag each trace dump file as being "notified," so you don't get a mail message sent to you every five minutes. The "notified" flag will be reset once each day, so that one message will be sent every day until the DBA takes corrective action based upon the contents of the trace dump file.

For each trace dump file that was created as the result of a user invoking the SQL Trace operation, the script will do the following:

- Rename the **.trc* trace dump file to **.ttt*

- Set the file's permission to be world-readable

- Delete the file once it is three days old

This script also handles Oracle alert files, by creating a new "version" of the alert log file on a daily basis (always retaining a week's worth of alert logs for subsequent review). This process will automatically operate for each database on the system.

The *every5* script is the main script used to check for any database errors. It is executed every five minutes as a *cron* job, and you can easily modify it to add your own site-specific filtering rules.

The following scripts are also called by the *every5* script:

days_old

Returns the number of days the specified file has existed. Used by the *every5* script to detect the age of the alert log file.

mailto

Mails contents of the specified text or file to the DBA. This script is called by many of the previous scripts to notify the DBA of any errors. This script is site-specific; edit the file to include your mail address.

mktemp

Substitute "mktemp" command for UNIX systems that do not have a *mktemp* command, in order to create a temporary scratch file. Called by the *every5* and *is_dbo* scripts to calculate a unique temporary file name.

Implementation details

To schedule this script to run automatically by using the UNIX *cron* facility, follow these steps:

1. Place all of these files in a directory in your PATH.

2. Edit the *mailto* file, specifying the desired email address(es) to which to send DBA notification mail messages.

3. Make sure that all of these files have the UNIX "rwx" permission.

4. Edit a file called *crontab.dat* containing the following line,

   ```
   0,5,10,15,20,25,30,35,40,45,50,55 * * * * /p/every5 > /p/every5.log
   ```

   where "/p" is the path of the *every5* script file.

5. Schedule the *every5* script file to run every five minutes by typing:

   ```
   crontab crontab.dat
   ```

   Note that this will replace any previous *crontab* list of jobs with the single *every5* job. To preserve the existing jobs, use "*crontab -l*" to list all of the existing jobs to a file, and include those existing jobs in the newly created *crontab.dat* file.

Restrictions

- The *oratab* file must exists in */etc* or */var/opt/oracle*.

- The ORACLE_BASE environment variable must be defined.

- An OFA-compliant directory structure is required (so that a database's background and user dump file destinations can be located); OFA is the Optimal Flexible Architecture, as documented by Oracle Corporation.

- The *days_old, mailto, mktemp,* and *oraenv* scripts must be found in the PATH.

- The *$HOME/dbabatch* script must exist.

locks

Directory: *$TOOLS*
File Type: Shell Script
Edit Required: No
Output File: Screen
Syntax: locks *[sid]*

sid

> The Oracle SID of the database whose locks are to be displayed. If omitted, the value of the ORACLE_SID environment variable will be used.

This script creates a report of all of the existing locks (if any) for a given database.

Nonprivileged users can be granted access to this script. In this way, application developers can view the locks their applications have imposed on the database without needing to involve the DBA. See the comments within the script for further information.

Restrictions

- The *define* and *fixcase* scripts must exist and be found in the PATH.

- The *$TOOLS/locks.sql* script must exist.

Sample report

```
                       Lock report for the DEV database


     -----O/S------ -----ORACLE-----                               Lock
     Username   Pid Username  ID  Ser Type        Object Name   Lock Held Requested
     ------------- ---------------- ----------  ---------------- --------- ---------
     oracle   18183 OPS$ORAC   6  372 Trans                                Exclusive
     oracle   18139 OPS$ORAC   7  240 Trans       (Rollback=R01) Exclusive
     oracle   18139 OPS$ORAC   7  240 DML         PRODUCT        Row Excl
     oracle   18183 OPS$ORAC   6  372 DML         PRODUCT        Row Share
```

This report shows that the process with the ID of 6 is requesting an exclusive lock on the PRODUCT object, but the process with the ID of 7 is already holding an exclusive lock on the PRODUCT object. Process ID 6 is locked, waiting for process ID 7 to release its exclusive lock.

locks.sql

Directory: *$TOOLS*
File Type: SQL Script
Edit Required: No
Output File: *locks.lis*

This script is called by the *locks* script to create the report described in the previous section.

validate

Directory: *$DBA*
File Type: SQL Script
Edit Required: No
Output File: Screen
Syntax: validate *sid*

sid
    The Oracle SID of the database to be validated.

This script creates and then executes an ANALYZE VALIDATE STRUCTURE on all tables (and their related indexes) for the database specified in the $1 parameter. (Note that in a small database, the validation process may only take a few minutes to complete.)

The *$DBA/validate.sql* script (see the next section) is executed to create the required validation script file.

Restrictions

* The *define, fixcase,* and *valid_db* scripts must exist and be found in the PATH.

* The *$DBA/validate.sql* script must exist.

validate.sql

Directory: *$DBA*
File Type: SQL Script
Edit Required: No
Output File: *validate_<sid>.sql*

This script is executed by the *validate* script to create the validation script file described in the previous section.

5

Database Security Reports and Utilities

Security features control and monitor access to a database and its objects. Such monitoring is important because it protects valuable data from unwarranted access or modification. DBAs must periodically examine, evaluate, and reevaluate users' access to the database's objects.

To avoid having to create and administer database passwords, OPS$ accounts. may be created. These accounts are especially useful in batch job script files; with these accounts you can avoid having to include passwords in the script files, thereby creating security problems.

The scripts described in this chapter create security reports for database grants, profiles, quotas, roles, and user accounts. You can create auditing reports by user and object over time, easily duplicate user accounts, and readily create OPS$ accounts.

allgrant

Directory: *$DBA*
File Type: Shell Script
Edit Required: No
Output File: *allgrant.lst*

This script creates a report of the direct grants made against all tables, views, and programs segregated by the type of the grant recipient. This report is a complete listing of all methods by which all objects may be accessed. It can be used to research the potential impact of revokes against objects that have multiple access paths that lead to it.

The script will prompt for the Oracle SID of the database to be accessed.

Sample report

```
allgrant - Direct Grants made to all objects
```

Lvl	OWNER	TABLE_NAME	GRANTEE	PRIVILEGE
Pub	ABMS	SPECIALTIES	PUBLIC	SELECT
Pub	DDW	CORP_TT	PUBLIC	SELECT
Pub	DDWMD	AGENTS	PUBLIC	DELETE
Pub	DDWMD	AGENTS	PUBLIC	INSERT
Pub	DDWMD	AGENTS	PUBLIC	SELECT
Pub	DDWMD	AGENTS	PUBLIC	UPDATE
Pub	DDWMD	AGENT_PROP	PUBLIC	DELETE
Pub	DDWMD	AGENT_PROP	PUBLIC	INSERT
Pub	DDWMD	AGENT_PROP	PUBLIC	SELECT
Pub	DDWMD	AGENT_PROP	PUBLIC	UPDATE
Role	EWEISS	CDAPI	CKR_EWEISS	EXECUTE
Role	EWEISS	CDBH_FHRG	CKR_EWEISS	EXECUTE
Role	EWEISS	CDBLS	CKR_EWEISS	EXECUTE
Role	EWEISS	CDBL_ELEMENT	CKR_EWEISS	DELETE
Role	EWEISS	CDBL_ELEMENT	CKR_EWEISS	INSERT
Role	EWEISS	CDBL_ELEMENT	CKR_EWEISS	SELECT
Role	EWEISS	CDBL_ELEMENT	CKR_EWEISS	UPDATE
Role	EWEISS	CDBL_OPERATIONS	CKR_EWEISS	DELETE
Role	EWEISS	CDBL_OPERATIONS	CKR_EWEISS	INSERT
Role	EWEISS	CDBL_OPERATIONS	CKR_EWEISS	SELECT
Role	EWEISS	CDBL_OPERATIONS	CKR_EWEISS	UPDATE
User	FOSBORN	CDRF_TMP_TBL	ALEX	DELETE
User	FOSBORN	CDRF_TMP_TBL	ALEX	INSERT
User	FOSBORN	CDRF_TMP_TBL	ALEX	SELECT
User	FOSBORN	CDRF_TMP_TBL	ALEX	UPDATE
User	FOSBORN	CDRK_TMP_TBL	ALEX	DELETE
User	FOSBORN	CDRK_TMP_TBL	ALEX	INSERT
User	FOSBORN	CDRK_TMP_TBL	ALEX	SELECT
User	FOSBORN	CDRK_TMP_TBL	ALEX	UPDATE
User	FOSBORN	CI_TABLE_DEFINITIONS	ALEX	DELETE
User	FOSBORN	CI_TABLE_DEFINITIONS	ALEX	INSERT
User	FOSBORN	CI_TABLE_DEFINITIONS	ALEX	SELECT
User	FOSBORN	CI_TABLE_DEFINITIONS	ALEX	UPDATE
User	FOSBORN	CKUXX	ALEX	EXECUTE
User	SYS	DBMS_DEFER_IMPORT_INTERNAL	SYSTEM	EXECUTE
User	SYS	DBMS_LOCK	EWEISS	EXECUTE
User	SYS	DBMS_LOCK	FOSBORN	EXECUTE
User	SYS	DBMS_ORACLE_TRACE_AGENT	TRACESVR	EXECUTE
User	SYS	DBMS_PIPE	EWEISS	EXECUTE
User	SYS	DBMS_PIPE	FOSBORN	EXECUTE

allgrant.sql

Directory: *$DBA*
File Type: SQL Script
Edit Required: No
Output File: *allgrant.lst*

This script is called by the *allgrant* script to create the report described in the previous section.

allprivs

Directory: *$DBA*
File Type: Shell Script
Edit Required: No
Output File: Screen

This script creates a report of the direct grants made to all users and roles. It lists all of the direct grants made to all users and roles, segregated by the nature of the grant. The script will prompt for the Oracle SID of the database to be accessed.

Sample report

```
allprivs - All Direct Grants
```

Level	PRIVILEGE	Gtbl	OWNER	Table Name
Column	UPDATE	NO	SYSTEM	TOOL_DEPENDENT
Role	CKR_EWEISS	YES		
Role	CKR_FOSBORN	NO		
Role	CKR_FOSBORN	YES		
Role	CONNECT	NO		
Role	CONNECT	YES		
Role	DBA	NO		
Role	DBA	YES		
Sys Priv	ALTER ANY CLUSTER	YES		
Sys Priv	ALTER ANY INDEX	YES		
Sys Priv	ALTER ANY PROCEDURE	YES		
Sys Priv	ALTER ANY ROLE	YES		
Table	EXECUTE	NO	EWEISS	CIOMODULE_DETAIL_COLUMN_USAGE
Table	EXECUTE	NO	EWEISS	CIOMODULE_DETAIL_TABLE_USAGE
Table	EXECUTE	NO	EWEISS	CIOMODULE_FUNCTION
Table	INSERT	NO	EWEISS	RM$HASHES
Table	INSERT	NO	EWEISS	RM$HASH_ELMS
Table	INSERT	NO	EWEISS	RM$HASH_TLG
Table	INSERT	NO	EWEISS	RM$NLS_DATA_TYPE_VALUES
Table	INSERT	NO	EWEISS	RM$NLS_ELEMENT_TYPES
Table	REFERENCES	NO	WEB2	FUEL_DRV_SUM

Table	REFERENCES	NO	WEB2	FUEL_EXCEPTIONS
Table	REFERENCES	NO	WEB2	FUEL_MASTER
Table	REFERENCES	NO	WEB2	FUEL_VEH_SUM
Table	REFERENCES	NO	WEB2	HOLIDAY
Table	SELECT	NO	FOSBORN	CDI_CODE_SECTION_TYPES
Table	SELECT	NO	FOSBORN	CDI_DEFINITION_VERSION
Table	SELECT	NO	FOSBORN	CDI_DELTAB
Table	SELECT	NO	FOSBORN	CDI_DFLT_USER_PREFS
Table	SELECT	NO	FOSBORN	CDI_DFLT_USER_PREF_USAGES
Table	SELECT	NO	FOSBORN	CDI_DICTIONARY_VERSION
Table	SELECT	NO	FOSBORN	CDI_FORMS
Table	SELECT	NO	FOSBORN	CDI_FUNNET
Table	SELECT	NO	FOSBORN	CDI_GENERATION_TARGETS
Table	SELECT	NO	FOSBORN	CDI_GEN_TARGET_PROPERTIES
Table	SELECT	NO	FOSBORN	CDI_HELP_TEXT

allprivs.sql

Directory: *$DBA*
File Type: SQL Script
Edit Required: No
Output File: *allprivs.lst*

This script is called by the *allprivs* script to create the desired report, as described in the previous section.

alltabp

Directory: *$DBA*
File Type: Shell Script
Edit Required: No
Output File: Screen

This script creates a report of all grants to all tables. It lists all table privileges made to all users and roles. The script will prompt for the Oracle SID of the database to be accessed.

Sample report

```
alltabp - All Table Privileges

Grantor    Grantee    Table Name                           Privilege Owner     Grant
---------  ---------  -----------------------------------  --------- --------- ---
ABMS       PUBLIC     SPECIALTIES                          SELECT
DDW        PUBLIC     CORP_TT                              SELECT
DDWMD      PUBLIC     AGENTS                               DELETE
                                                           INSERT
                                                           UPDATE
                                                           SELECT
```

		AGENT_PROP	DELETE
			INSERT
			UPDATE
			SELECT
EWEISS	CKR_EWEISS	CDAPI	EXECUTE
		CDBH_FHRG	EXECUTE
		CDBLS	EXECUTE
		CDBL_ELEMENT	DELETE
			INSERT
			SELECT
			UPDATE
POB	PUBLIC	WDE	EXECUTE
POB2	PUBLIC	WDE	EXECUTE
POBTEST	ORAWEB	ACCOUNT_FUNCTION	SELECT
		ACCT_MASTER	SELECT
		CREDIT	SELECT
		CUSTOMER	SELECT
		CUSTOMER_PROFILE	SELECT
		T_ACCT_MASTER	SELECT
	POB	ACCOUNT_FUNCTION	SELECT
		ACCT_MASTER	SELECT
		CREDIT	SELECT
		CUSTOMER	SELECT
		CUSTOMER_PROFILE	SELECT
SYS	EWEISS	DBMS_LOCK	EXECUTE
		DBMS_PIPE	EXECUTE
	FOSBORN	DBMS_LOCK	EXECUTE
		DBMS_PIPE	EXECUTE
YORK	PUBLIC	SFR_TEMPLATE	SELECT

alltab.sql

Directory: *$DBA*
File Type: SQL Script
Edit Required: No
Output File: *alltabp.lis*

This script is called by the *alltabp* script to create the desired report, as described previously.

audses.sql

Directory: *$DBA*
File Type: SQL Script
Edit Required: No
Output File: *audses.lst*

This script creates an audit report of the current month's usage by username.

auditobj.sql

Directory: *$DBA*
File Type: SQL Script
Edit Required: No
Output File: *auditobj.lst*

This script creates a report of all of the object auditing options that are currently in effect in this database.

auditst.sql

Directory: *$DBA*
File Type: SQL Script
Edit Required: No
Output File: *auditst.lst*

This script creates a report of all of the statement auditing options that are currently in effect in this database.

audobj.sql

Directory: *$DBA*
File Type: SQL Script
Edit Required: No
Output File: *audobj.lst*

This script creates a report of all of the statement and object auditing records.

audhot.sql

Directory: *$DBA*
File Type: SQL Script
Edit Required: No
Output File: *audhot.lis*

This script creates a report of the tables and views for the objects that are most frequently accessed, thereby consuming the most system I/O resources. Note that table auditing must be initialized in order for this script to function.

colgrant

Directory: *$DBA*
File Type: Shell Script
Edit Required: No
Output File: Screen

This script creates a report of all of the direct grants made against all columns of a specific table or view. This report is a complete listing of all methods by which the columns may be accessed. It can be used to research the potential impact of revokes against columns that have multiple access paths that lead to it.

The script will prompt for the Oracle SID of the database to be accessed, the schema name that owns the table or view, and the table or view name to be accessed.

Sample report

```
COLGRANT - Direct Grants made on cols to TOOL_DEPENDENT for dev
```

COLUMN_NAME	Level	GRANTEE	PRIVILEGE	Gtbl
DEPCHANGED	Public	PUBLIC	UPDATE	NO

colgrant.sql

Directory: *$DBA*
File Type: SQL Script
Edit Required: No
Output File: *colgrant.lst*

This script is called by the *colgrant* script to create the list of grants, as described in the previous section.

copyuser

Directory: *$DBA*
File Type: Shell Script
Edit Required: No
Output File: Screen
Syntax: copyuser *sid username newuser*

sid

    The Oracle SID of the database to be accessed.

username

The name of the existing user ID from which to copy.

newuser

The new user ID to be created.

This script allows you to easily copy all of the information about an existing user to a new user.

Often, when users ask for another user ID in the database, they say "just make it like the ID xxxxxxx." This can involve a highly manual-intensive process that is subject to errors, even when using roles.

This script will create a new user that matches the account associated with an existing user.

Restrictions

- This script requires the following files to exist:

  $DBA/copyusg.sql
  $DBA/copyusis.sql
  $DBA/copyusl.sql
  $DBA/copyustg.sql
  $DBA/copyuser.sql
  $DBA/define
  $DBA/fixcase
  $DBA/valid_db

- An OPS$username account must exist (where username matches your UNIX operating system username). This account can be created by executing the *creops* script.

- The PWSYS environment variable must exist. This variable must contain the password to the Oracle database's SYS account.

creops

Directory: *$DBA*
File Type: Shell Script
Edit Required: No
Output File: Screen
Syntax: `creops` *sid*

sid

Oracle SID of the database in which to create the new account.

This script creates an OPS$username account (where username is your current username) in the database whose SID is specified as a parameter. It copies the security from the SYSTEM account to the new OPS$username account, in order to create an exact duplicate of all of the granted privileges and specifications in the new account.

If an OPS$username account exists, you can easily log into the database without having to specify a username or password. Here is an example for SQL*Plus:

```
sqlplus /
```

Restrictions

- The *creops* script requires that the following files exist:

  $DBA/copyusg.sql
  $DBA/copyusis.sql
  $DBA/copyusl.sql
  $DBA/copyustg.sql
  $DBA/copyuser.sql
  $TOOLS/define
  $TOOLS/fixcase
  $DBA/valid_db

- An OPS$username account must exist (where username matches your UNIX operating system username).

- The PWSYS environment variable must exist. This variable must contain the password to the Oracle database's SYS account.

- The PW environment variable must exist. This variable must contain the password to the Oracle database's SYSTEM account.

getgrant.sql

Directory: *$DBA*
File Type: SQL Script
Edit Required: No
Output File: *regrant.sql*

This script creates another script that will contain the grant statements necessary to regenerate the table-level and column-level grants for a specified table, when that table is recreated.

grant_to

Directory: *$DBA*
File Type: Shell Script
Edit Required: No
Output File: Screen

This script creates a report of all of the direct grants made to a specific user or role. It lists all of the direct grants made to a specific user or role, segregated by the nature of the grant. This report is a complete listing of all initial permissions along all access paths for a user. The script can be used to research the potential impact of revoking any direct grant issued to a user or role.

The script will prompt for the Oracle SID of the database to be accessed, and the user name or role for which to report the direct grants.

Sample report

```
GRANT_TO - Direct Grants made to POB


Level      PRIVILEGE        Gtbl OWNER     Table Name                  Col Name
--------   ---------------  ---- --------- --------------------------  ----------
Role       CONNECT          NO
Role       RESOURCE         NO
Sys Priv   UNLIMITED TABLE  NO
           SPACE

Table      SELECT           NO   POBTEST   ACCOUNT_FUNCTION
Table      SELECT           NO   POBTEST   ACCT_MASTER
Table      SELECT           NO   POBTEST   CREDIT
Table      SELECT           NO   POBTEST   CUSTOMER
Table      SELECT           NO   POBTEST   CUSTOMER_PROFILE
```

The above report shows that the POB user has the following:

- CONNECT and RESOURCE privileges granted to it via a role
- The UNLIMITED TABLESPACE privilege directly granted to it
- SELECT access to five specific tables

grant_to.sql

Directory: *$DBA*
File Type: SQL Script
Edit Required: No
Output File: *grant_to.lis*

This script is called by the *grant_to* script to create the desired report, as described in the previous section.

grantall.sql

Directory: *$DBA*
File Type: SQL Script
Edit Required: No
Output File: *grall_tmp.sql, grall.sql*

This script creates and then executes a script to grant the specified username (such as OPS$ORACLE) all privileges to all nonsystem objects in a database.

grantool

Directory: *$DBA*
File Type: Shell Script
Edit Required: No
Output File: Screen

This script grants SELECT access on required tables to a specific user, for use in running the *$TOOLS/dbousers, $TOOLS/dbo_sql,* and *$TOOLS/locks* utilities.

Note that if this procedure has a privilege violation when trying to grant access to the V$ tables, you must first run the *grantsys.sql* script, which will grant SELECT WITH GRANT OPTION to yourself, and then rerun the *grantool* script.

The script will prompt for the Oracle SID of the database to be accessed, and the username to be granted SELECT access to the required tables.

grantool.sql

Directory: *$DBA*
File Type: SQL Script
Edit Required: No
Output File: Screen

This script is called by the *grantool* script to perform the actual grants, as described in the previous section.

grantsys.sql

Directory: *$DBA*
File Type: SQL Script
Edit Required: No
Output File: Screen

This script grants to the current user account the privileges required to grant other users access to the *$TOOLS/dbo* and *locks* utilities (via the *grantools* script).

You will use this script when your account (typically, OPS$oracle) does not have the SELECT privilege WITH GRANT OPTION on the required V$ tables. The script will prompt you for the SYS account password.

makeops

Directory: *$DBA*
File Type: Shell Script
Edit Required: No
Output File: Screen
Syntax: `makeops sid newuser`

sid
   The Oracle SID of the database to be accessed.

newuser
   The new User ID (less the "OPS$" prefix) to be created.

This script creates a new OPS$ username account for a given user, matching the configuration and privileges of the user's current non-OPS$ account. This allows the DBA to quickly create an OPS$ account for a given user which is otherwise identical to the user's existing account without having to determine and duplicate existing privileges. If an OPS$username account exists, the user can then easily log into the database without having to specify a username or password. Here is an example for SQL*Plus:

```
sqlplus /
```

The account is created with an "impossible" password, so that it can only be accessed from the server, and even then only by the sqlplus "/" clause.

Restrictions

- This script requires that the following files exist:

   $DBA/makeops.sql
   $DBA/copyusis.sql
   $TOOLS/define
   $TOOLS/fixcase
   $DBA/valid_db

- An OPS$username account must exist (where username matches your UNIX operating system username). This can be created by executing the *creops* script.

- The PWSYS environment variable must exist. This variable must contain the password to the Oracle database's SYS account.

- The PW environment variable must exist. This variable must contain the password to the Oracle database's SYSTEM account.

makeops.sql

Directory: *$DBA*
File Type: SQL Script
Edit Required: No
Output File: *makeops.tmp*

This script is called by the *makeops* script to create the script that will be used to create the new user account, as described in the previous section.

privlist

Directory: *$DBA*
File Type: SQL Script
Edit Required: No
Output File: Screen

The *privlist* script creates a report containing the security privilege objects along all access paths that exist for the specified user or role. The script does this by drilling through all levels of indirection. The script is used to determine a complete list of security privilege objects for a user. The source of each individual privilege is listed so that the proper REVOKE statement can be issued to deny the listed privileges.

The script will prompt for the Oracle SID of the database to be accessed, and the user or role name for which to report privileges.

privlist.sql

Directory: *$DBA*
File Type: SQL Script
Edit Required: No
Output File: *privlist.lst*

This script is called by the *privlist* script to create the desired report, as described in the previous section.

privs

Directory: *$DBA*
File Type: Shell Script
Edit Required: No
Output File: Screen

This script prints a privilege report for the specified user, listing the granted roles and the individual object privileges granted to the user or PUBLIC. This report is smaller than the one generated by the *privlist* script, since the granted roles do not have their privileges broken out, and the DELETE/INSERT/SELECT/UPDATE appear only once per table.

Sample report

```
Roles granted to JRSMITH in app


    GRANTED_ROLE
    ------------------------
    MATERIAL
    ORACLEUSER
    WAFPOSFLR


    Roles granted to PUBLIC in app

    GRANTED_ROLE
    ------------------------
    MONITORER


        (In PRIVILEGE column, D=Delete, I=Insert, S=Select, U=Update)


    Direct table grants to JRSMITH in app


    OWNER          TABLE_NAME                        PRIVILEGE   Admin
    ------------   ---------------------------       ----------- -----
    PROD1          WIPDATA                               S        nnnn
    PROD1          WIPSUMM                               S        nnnn


    Direct table grants to PUBLIC in app


    OWNER          TABLE_NAME                        PRIVILEGE   Admin
    ------------   ---------------------------       ----------- -----
    PROD1          LAYER_RECIPE                          S        nnnn
    PROD1          OPENWO                                S        nnnn
    PROD1          LIMIT_GROWTH                          S        nnnn
    PROD1          LIMIT_PROC1                           S        nnnn
    PROD1          LIMIT_PROC2                           S        nnnn
    PROD1          LIMIT_STRUCT1                         S        nnnn
    PROD1          LIMIT_STRUCT2                         S        nnnn
    PLU            PRT_BLOB                             DISU       nnnn
    PLU            PRT_LONG_ID                           S        nnnn
    PLU            PRT_LONG_TEXT                        DISU       nnnn
```

profiles

Directory: *$DBA*
File Type: Shell Script
Edit Required: No
Output File: Screen
Syntax: `profiles` *[sid]*

sid

> Optional Oracle SID for the database to be reported; if omitted, all databases will be reported.

This script creates a report of all profiles that are defined in the specified database (or all databases if a particular database is not specified).

profiles.sql

Directory: *$DBA*
File Type: SQL Script
Edit Required: No
Output File: *profiles.lst*

This script is called by the *profiles* script to create the desired report, as described in the prevous section.

Sample report

```
PROFILES - Profiles


Profile          Resource
Name             Name                       Limit
---------------  -------------------------  ---------------
DEFAULT          COMPOSITE_LIMIT            UNLIMITED
DEFAULT          SESSIONS_PER_USER          UNLIMITED
DEFAULT          CPU_PER_SESSION            UNLIMITED
DEFAULT          CPU_PER_CALL               UNLIMITED
DEFAULT          LOGICAL_READS_PER_SESSION  UNLIMITED
DEFAULT          LOGICAL_READS_PER_CALL     UNLIMITED
DEFAULT          IDLE_TIME                  UNLIMITED
DEFAULT          CONNECT_TIME               UNLIMITED
DEFAULT          PRIVATE_SGA                UNLIMITED

9 rows selected.
```

quotas

Directory: *$DBA*
File Type: Shell Script
Edit Required: No
Output File: Screen
Syntax: quotas *[sid]*

sid

> Optional Oracle SID for the database to be reported; if omitted, all databases will be reported.

This script creates a report of all user account quotas that are defined in the specified database (or all databases if a particular database is not specified).

Sample report

```
                 QUOTAS - Database User Quotas

              Tablespace       MB      Max MB
USERNAME      Name             Quota   Quota
------------- ---------------- ------  ---------
ABMS          TEMPORARY_DATA   0       unlimited
              USER_DATA        61016   unlimited
ALEX          DES2             2600    unlimited
              TEMPORARY_DATA   0       unlimited
ALLIED        TEMPORARY_DATA   0       unlimited
              USER_DATA        0       unlimited
CANYORK       TEMPORARY_DATA   0       unlimited
              USER_DATA        54002   unlimited
CRUISE        TEMPORARY_DATA   0       unlimited
              USER_DATA        580     unlimited
CULLIGAN      TEMPORARY_DATA   0       unlimited
              USER_DATA        21620   unlimited
DDWMD         TEMPORARY_DATA   0       76800
              USERS            0       unlimited
              USER_DATA        42780   76800
EWEISS        TEMPORARY_DATA   0       unlimited
              USER_DATA        21694   unlimited
FOSBORN       TEMPORARY_DATA   0       unlimited
              USER_DATA        0       unlimited
LOCATOR       TEMPORARY_DATA   0       unlimited
              USER_DATA        18720   unlimited
MARVIN        TEMPORARY_DATA   0       unlimited
              USER_DATA        2900    unlimited
MDSYS         SYSTEM           190     unlimited
OPS$DHARRIS   USER_DATA        360     unlimited
```

quotas.sql

Directory: *$DBA*
File Type: SQL Script
Edit Required: No
Output File: *quotas.lst*

This script is called by the *quotas* script to create the desired report, as described in the previous section.

readonly.sql

Directory: *$DBA*
File Type: SQL Script
Edit Required: No
Output File: Screen

This script is used to grant SELECT access to each non-SYS/non-SYSTEM/non-OPS$-owned table, view, and snapshot to the READONLY role. It can be used to eliminate the need to grant the SELECT ANY TABLE privilege to users.

You should reexecute this script whenever a new table, view, or snapshot is created (or on a periodic basis, such as a nightly batch job to ensure that any new tables, views, or snapshots created that day are found).

Restrictions

- Before running this script, the DBA must create the READONLY role and grant it CONNECT privilege. For example:

```
create role readonly;
grant connect to readonly;
```

- There must be an existing OPS$username account, having DBA privileges. For example:

```
create user ops$oracle identified externally temporary tablespace temp;
grant connect, resource, dba to ops$oracle;
```

rolelist

Directory: *$DBA*
File Type: Shell Script
Edit Required: No
Output File: Screen

This script creates a report of all of the roles in the database and to whom (user or role) they were granted. This report is used to walk backwards along all access paths in the database to their start points (usernames). It can be used when researching the levels of security indirection in a database.

The script assumes that the Oracle SID of the database to be accessed has been set via the *define* script.

Sample report

```
ROLELIST - List of all roles
```

ROLE	Password Protected	GRANTEE	Admin Option	Default Role?
CKR_EWEISS	NO	EWEISS	YES	YES
CKR_FOSBORN	NO	ALEX	NO	YES
CKR_FOSBORN	NO	FOSBORN	YES	YES
CONNECT	NO	ABMS	NO	YES
CONNECT	NO	ABMS2	NO	YES
CONNECT	NO	ALEX	NO	YES
CONNECT	NO	ALLIED	NO	YES
DBA	NO	SYS	YES	YES
DBA	NO	SYSTEM	YES	YES
EXP_FULL_DATABASE	NO	DBA	NO	YES
EXP_FULL_DATABASE	NO	SYS	YES	YES
IMP_FULL_DATABASE	NO	DBA	NO	YES
IMP_FULL_DATABASE	NO	SYS	YES	YES
RESOURCE	NO	SYS	YES	YES

rolelist.sql

Directory: *$DBA*
File Type: SQL Script
Edit Required: No
Output File: *rolelist.lst*

This script is called by the *rolelist* script to create the desired report, as described in the previous section.

tabgrant

Directory: *$DBA*
File Type: SQL Script
Edit Required: No
Output File: Screen

This script creates a report of all direct grants made against a specific table, view, or program object, segregated by the type of the grant recipient. The report is a complete listing of all methods by which the object may be accessed. It can be used to research the potential impact of revokes against objects that have multiple access paths that lead to it.

The script will prompt for the Oracle SID of the database to be accessed, and the schema name that owns the table, view, or program object.

Sample report

```
TABGRANT - Direct Grants made to SDD_ELEMENTS

Level    GRANTEE                    PRIVILEGE                   Gtbl
-------  -------------------------  --------------------------  ----
Role     CKR_FOSBORN                DELETE                      NO
Role     CKR_FOSBORN                INSERT                      NO
Role     CKR_FOSBORN                SELECT                      NO
Role     CKR_FOSBORN                UPDATE                      NO
User     ALEX                       DELETE                      NO
User     ALEX                       INSERT                      NO
User     ALEX                       SELECT                      NO
User     ALEX                       UPDATE                      NO
```

The above report shows that the CKR_FOSBORN role and the ALEX user account have been granted the DELETE, INSERT, SELECT, and UPDATE privileges on this table.

tabgrant.sql

Directory: *$DBA*
File Type: SQL Script
Edit Required: No
Output File: *tabgrant.lst*

This script is called by the *tabgrant* script to create the desired report, as described in the previous section.

usrs

Directory: *$DBA*
File Type: SQL Script
Edit Required: No
Output File: *usrs.lst*
Syntax: usrs *[sid]*

sid

> The Oracle SID for the database; if omitted, the user accounts for all databases will be reported.

This script creates a report of all user accounts that are defined in the specified database (or all databases if a particular database is not specified).

The script will prompt for the Oracle SID of the database to be accessed.

Sample report

```
                          USRS - Database Users


                      Default     Temporary
USERNAME          ID  Tablespace  Tablespace   Profile               CREATED
---------------- ---- ----------- ------------ -------------------- ---------
SYS                0  SYSTEM      TEMPORARY    DEFAULT              08-JAN-97
SYSTEM             5  TOOLS       TEMPORARY    DEFAULT              08-JAN-97
MCALISI           11  USER_DATA   TEMPORARY    DEFAULT              08-JAN-97
TRACESVR           8  SYSTEM      TEMPORARY    DEFAULT              08-JAN-97
MDSYS              9  SYSTEM      TEMPORARY    DEFAULT              08-JAN-97
HERMAN            10  USER_DATA   TEMPORARY    DEFAULT              08-JAN-97
WEB2              14  USER_DATA   TEMPORARY    DEFAULT              15-JAN-97
RYDER             51  USER_DATA   TEMPORARY    DEFAULT              11-JUN-97
CULLIGAN          53  USER_DATA   TEMPORARY    DEFAULT              19-JUN-97
TETRAULT          54  USER_DATA   TEMPORARY    DEFAULT              01-JUL-97
ABMS2             55  USER_DATA   TEMPORARY    DEFAULT              01-JUL-97
DDW               58  USER_DATA   TEMPORARY    DEFAULT              31-JUL-97
OPS$ORACLE        56  SYSTEM      SYSTEM       DEFAULT              09-JUL-97
```

usrs.sql

Directory: *$DBA*

File Type: SQL Script

Edit Required: No

Output File: *usrs.lst*

This script is called by the *usrs* script to create the desired report, as described in the previous section.

Database Backup
Utilities

A recent study performed by the Educational Testing Service to define objectively the job of Oracle database administrators found that the single most important task performed by the DBA is database backup and recovery. Most DBAs agree: there is nothing more important than protecting the contents of the database.

Planning and executing a backup and recovery strategy is a detailed and time-consuming process. It is critical that the backup be performed properly, since even the smallest error or omission may result in an unrecoverable database. On the accompanying CD-ROM we provide a set of highly sophisticated and powerful scripts that will allow you to quickly implement a "bulletproof" backup and recovery strategy—one that can be easily tailored to your own specific environment.

Without a robust backup policy and procedure in place, sites risk losing the valuable data contained within the database whenever an unexpected error, such as a media or other hardware failure, occurs.

The scripts described in this chapter provide comprehensive cold and hot backup solutions for an Oracle database running on a UNIX platform, as well as an optional full export of the database. The backup scripts contain complete error trapping and notification to detect and report any backup failures.

NOTE   These scripts were originally developed on HP-UX and Pyramid platforms. Because most UNIX environments are unique, you may need to change these scripts so they will function properly on your system. If you are modifying them for a non-UNIX system, see the "Converting to Other Operating Systems" section in Chapter 1, *Introduction.*

Installation and Configuration

NOTE   This sample installation is configured for a database instance named PROD. You will need to change all references to PROD to the Oracle System Identifier (SID) of the database that is the target of the backup. See the individual script descriptions for more information regarding any required or optional customizations.

The instructions in this section assume that you have already installed the scripts from the CD-ROM provided with this book. If you have not yet done so, go to the "Installing the Scripts" section in Chapter 1, and follow the instructions there.

The following steps install and configure the backup scripts on your system. These steps assume that the $HOME, $TOOLS, and $DBA environment variables have been defined, and that the corresponding directories have been created with appropriate privileges.

1. Copy the *dbabatch* file to your *$HOME* directory.

2. Copy the following files to the *$DBA* directory (note that the file names are case-sensitive) if they are not already there:

allmemry
allmemry.c
archwait.sql
backarch
backcln
backdisp
backprod
backprod.dat
backup
calcbkup
ccontrol
ccontrol.sql
chkcm.sql
copy_log
crearch
creback
creback.sql
dbakill.c
dbo_stat
dbostart
dbostop

delarch
delarch2
fix_bkup
fix_rest
is_mgr
killunix
offline
online
rest_log
startm
startnet
stopm
stopnet

3. Copy the following files to the *$TOOLS* directory (note that the file names are case-sensitive) if they are not already there:

database
database.doc
dbousers
dbousers.sql
define
fixcase
getsyi
is_dbo
mailto
mktemp
replpath
trunc
valid_db

4. Rename the *$DBA/backprod.dat* file (see step 11 below).

5. Rename the *$DBA/backprod* file (see step 15 below).

6. Edit *$TOOLS/mailto* to set the desired email addresses to which to send errors. (See the notes in the *mailto* script for details.)

7. Edit *$TOOLS/fixcase* for your specific environment's ORACLE_SID case standards. (See the notes in the *fixcase* script for details.)

8. The *backup* script will display the amount of memory that is used at various times during the backup. This display will help you diagnose subsequent errors if available memory usage is too small. The HP-UX-specific *$DBA/allmemry* script compiles the *allmemry.c* source code into *$DBA/allmemry.exe*. The source code is only guaranteed to compile on HP-UX 9 or HP-UX 10. On

other platforms, substitute your own memory report or change the *$DBA/all-memry.c* source. (If you do not compile the *allmemry.c* source code, the *backup* script will ignore the memory checks.)

You can delete *$DBA/allmemry* and *$DBA/allmemry.c* if you are not using these files.

9. Create a list of all valid Oracle SIDs on your system. This list must be stored in a file called *$TOOLS/database*. A sample *$TOOLS/database* file is provided as an example. Instructions on how to edit this file are contained in the *$TOOLS/database.doc* file.

10. If you are backing up directly to a tape device, and *not* calling a third-party UNIX backup utility to perform the backup, edit *$DBA/backup* to change the tape device name to be used (the default is */dev/rmt/0m*).

11. If you are backing up directly to disk filesystem(s) (i.e., "disk-to-disk"), the backup script will back up all of the Oracle database *<sid>* files to a filesystem called */backup_<sid>* unless a *$DBA/back<sid>.dat* file is found. Delete or rename the *backPROD.dat* file if you are not using a backup override data file for the PROD database.

TIP

Many UNIX systems have a restriction that limits a filesystem's maximum size to four gigabytes. If your database is larger than four gigabytes, you will have to create multiple filesystems, called */backup_<sid>n* (where *n* is any unique digit), to contain the backed-up database files. In order for the backup scripts to know where to copy the files of your database, you must create a file called *$DBA/back<sid>.dat,* which contains the mapping of the UNIX root-level directories to the */backup_<sid>n* filesystems that will contain the backed-up database files. (For example, if you indicate that */u01* is associated with */backupPROD1*, then all files for database PROD that are located anywhere in the */u01* directory tree will be backed up to */backupPROD1*.)

You can indicate that multiple */unn* filesystems be mapped to a specific backup directory, although you must ensure that no more than four gigabytes of database files be backed up to one backup directory. The backup routine checks for the existence of this file, and will use it if it exists.

A sample *backPROD.dat* file is included in the list of files.

Ensure that the filesystems are sized large enough to contain all of the files that will be copied to them, and that the "oracle" owner can write to them.

---

12. Edit *$DBA/copy_log* to include all of your site-specific backup commands. (See the instructions contained in copy_log for details). *This is always*

required if you are using a site-specific "hot batch" backup method. (See the notes in the *copy_log* script for details.)

13. If you are performing cold backups, compile *$DBA/dbakill.c* so that *$DBA/kill-unix* will run properly. (See the instructions inside the *dbakill.c* script for details. Note that this operation will require root privileges.)

14. In order for the backup of archive logs to work properly, you may need to modify several *INIT.ORA* parameters as follows:

    LOG_ARCHIVE_DEST

    > Must include the prefix of the archive logs that will be written. The %s, %t, %S, or %T variables must not be specified in LOG_ARCHIVE_DEST; they can only be specified in LOG_ARCHIVE_FORMAT.

    LOG_ARCHIVE_FORMAT

    > Must contain the remainder of the archive log file specification. The %s, %t, %S, and %T variables can be specified in LOG_ARCHIVE_FORMAT.

    For example:

    ```
    LOG_ARCHIVE_FORMAT = _%s.ARC
    LOG_ARCHIVE_DEST = /oracle/archive/PROD/arc
    ```

    In this example, "*arc*" is the prefix of the archive files that will be written.

15. The *backup* script is usually executed nightly by a *cron* job, which executes the *$DBA/back<sid>* file that, in turn, executes the *$DBA/backup* script. A sample *backPROD* file is included. This file must be edited to include all of the *backup* parameters that pertain to the database being backed up; see the notes in the *$DBA/backup* script for parameter information.

Backup Methods

The backup scripts provide five basic methods of backing up an Oracle database. The following sections provide descriptions of the basic flow and operation of the scripts that implement each of these backup scenarios, with dependencies and decision points indicated.

NOTE   The scripts provided with this book display a lot of debugging information. This additional information can be invaluable in case the script fails to perform a proper backup as expected. Without this information, it may be impossible to determine the reason why a previous backup has failed. Aside from its use in case of backup failure, you can ignore the additional debugging information.

Cold backup to a system tape device

This method requires that the database be shut down. It then copies all database files to the backup device. When the database is running in NOARCHIVELOG mode, cold backup is the only backup method available. Note that such a cold backup can be used only to recover the entire database to its state at the time of the shutdown and subsequent backup. Any changes after that time will be lost.

Cold backup to disk

This method is similar to a cold backup to a system tape device, but in this case the database files are copied directly to one or more additional disk devices. This method will generally be faster than backup to tape, but it lacks the ability to save multiple generations of backups and to store the backup data offsite.

Hot backup to a system tape device

A hot backup allows the database to be backed up while it is up and running. This method is particularly useful for an installation where the database must be running 24 hours a day, and where there is no opportunity to shut down the database for backup. In addition, a hot backup may be used to back up a single tablespace at a time, which allows critical data to be backed up more often than other, more static data.

Hot backup to disk

This method is similar to the hot backup to tape, but as with the cold backup to disk, the database files are copied to one or more disk devices rather than to tape. While faster than backup to tape, this method does not permit multiple copies of the backup or offsite storage of the backup set.

Hot backup to a third-party device

As the size of a database gets larger and larger (often growing to hundreds of gigabytes), it becomes impractical to back up the database to standard system tape devices. This is a result of both capacity and speed limitations. To solve this problem, several vendors have developed backup devices that incorporate high speed, large capacity tape devices that have been specifically optimized for backup and recovery operations. On the accompanying CD-ROM, we provide a set of scripts to utilize a backup system from Alexandria Systems, which is one of the more common backup systems used with Oracle databases today. You can modify these scripts for backup systems from other vendors.

Cold Backup to Tape System Device

1. Verify that the required script parameters are present.

2. Ensure that the ORACLE_SID is in the proper case.

3. Parse the command input line for optional parameter(s).

4. Check for the "offline" flag (which will cause the backup for this database to be skipped). This is an easy way for the DBA to cause the backup for a specific database to skipped. The *offline* script sets the flag, while the *online* script clears the flag.

5. Verify the ORACLE_SID value against a list of all valid database SID values.

6. Execute the *define* script to define the ORACLE_BASE, ORACLE_HOME, ENVNAME, USERNAME, and APPL_TOP values, which are associated with the ORACLE_SID. (The ENVNAME, USERNAME, and APPL_TOP environment variables are used when the database is employed with Oracle Financial Applications; ENVNAME is the name of the application environment file, USERNAME is the username to use when executing Applications Object Library (AOL) calls for the database, and APPL_TOP is the application top directory associated with the specified database. These values, are not used if Oracle applications are not installed.) The *define* script calls the *replpath* script to ensure that one (and only one) ORACLE_HOME is present in the PATH.

7. Set the "offline" flag. (The existence of this flag can be used by other cooperating scripts to determine whether to allow other applications or scripts access to the database.) The included *menu* script is an example of a script that presents a menu of all available databases to a user; a database that is being backed up will remove itself from the menu (by setting the "offline" flag before the backup and clearing the "offline" flag after the backup is complete.)

8. If you are running Oracle Applications, display a list of any running concurrent manager processes (for debugging purposes).

9. Execute the *dbo_stat* script to determine whether the specified database is currently open. If the database is not running, the *dbostart* script is called to start up and open the database. (This is so that we can use SQL to build a backup script.)

10. Execute the *creback* script to build a SQL script which, when subsequently executed, will perform the backup of the database. Since the backup script is built from the current database structure, all of the existing database files will be automatically included in the backup. This ensures that no files are accidentally skipped, thereby invalidating the backup.

11. Execute the *crearch* script to create a variable containing the archive log destination if the database is running in ARCHIVELOG mode (so that any archive log files can be included in the backup).

12. Execute the *ccontrol* script to create a script that will recreate the control file for the database. This file will be included in the backup to provide an extra level of security, as well as to document all files and their locations.

13. If Oracle Applications are installed, execute the *dbousers* script to display a list of the current users (if any) in the database. This script calls the *allmemry* script (if it exists) to display the memory utilization before the concurrent managers are shut down, and calls the *stopmgr* script to shut down the concurrent manager processes.

14. Execute the *allmemry* script to display the memory utilization before the Oracle database is shut down.

15. Execute the *dbousers* script to display a list of the current users (if any) in the database, prior to its being shut down, for debugging purposes. UNIX processes accessing the database are also displayed.

16. If Oracle Applications are installed, execute the *killunix* script to try to kill the UNIX processes for any leftover concurrent manager jobs (that might not have properly shut down).

17. Execute the *dbousers* script again (for debugging purposes) to display a list of the current users (if any) that might still be accessing the database after the concurrent manager processes are killed.

18. Display a list of all database background processes and a list of the shared memory segments (for debugging purposes).

19. Execute the *dbostop* script to shut down the Oracle database. A list of any remaining UNIX processes that might be accessing the Oracle database is displayed for debugging purposes.

20. If Oracle Applications are installed, rename the standard concurrent manager log file to a filename ending in the 3-letter day of the week. This prevents the log file from continuously growing (eventually filling up the filesystem), keeps the last seven days of log files accessible on disk at all times for examination, and automatically purges old log data (since every new file replaces the corresponding file that was created seven days ago).

21. Display memory utilization statistics before the actual backup script executes, for debugging purposes.

22. Execute the previously-created backup script to perform the actual backup of the database to tape.

23. If the database is running in ARCHIVELOG mode, call the *backarch* script to back up any archive logs that might exist for the database as follows:

    — Call the *copy_log* script to copy the archive logs and the current control files to the backup tape.

    — Call the *delarch* script to delete all of the existing archive logs (since they are not needed anymore, now that the entire database has been successfully backed up). Because an active database can create one gigabyte or more of archive logs in a single day, it is important to routinely clean out the obsolete archive log files; the database will halt if the archive log file destination runs out of space.

24. If a full database export is specified (on the command line) take the following action:

    — Call the *dbostart* script to start the database in exclusive mode.

    — Execute the Oracle *exp* (Export) utility to perform a full export of the database to the tape device.

    — Display a list of database processes (for debugging).

    — Call the *dbostop* script to shut down the database.

25. Execute the *dbostart* script to start the database normally and clear the previously-set "offline" flag.

26. Execute the *allmemry* script to display the memory utilization statistics after the Oracle database is started.

27. If you are running Oracle Applications, call the *startmgr* script to start the standard concurrent manager process.

28. Display the ending time and exit.

Cold Backup to Disk

1. Verify that the required script parameters are present.

2. Ensure that the ORACLE_SID is in the proper case.

3. Parse the command input line for optional parameter(s).

4. Check for the "offline" flag (which will cause the backup for this database to be skipped). This is an easy way for the DBA to skip the backup for a specific database. The *offline* script sets the flag, while the *online* script clears the flag.

5. Verify the ORACLE_SID value against a list of all valid database SID values.

6. Execute the *define* script to define the ORACLE_BASE, ORACLE_HOME, ENVNAME, USERNAME, and APPL_TOP values, which are associated with

the ORACLE_SID. (The ENVNAME, USERNAME, and APPL_TOP environment variables are used when the database is employed with Oracle Financial Applications. ENVNAME is the name of the application environment file, USERNAME is the username to use when executing Applications Object Library (AOL) calls for the database, and APPL_TOP is the application top directory associated with the specified database. These values are not used if Oracle Applications are not installed.) The *define* script calls the *replpath* script to ensure that one (and only one) ORACLE_HOME is present in the PATH.

7. Set the "offline" flag. (The existence of this flag can be used by other cooperating scripts to determine whether to allow other applications or scripts access to the database. The included *menu* script is an example of a script that presents a menu of all available databases to a user; a database that is being backed up will remove itself from the menu by setting the "offline" flag before the backup and clearing the "offline" flag after the backup is complete.)

8. Execute the *calcbkup* script to calculate the desired filesystem, which will contain the database backup files.

9. If you are running Oracle Applications, display a list of any running concurrent manager processes (for debugging purposes).

10. Execute the *dbo_stat* script to determine whether the specified database is currently open. If the database is not running, call the *dbostart* script to start up and open the database so that SQL can be used to build a backup script.

11. Execute the *creback* script to build a SQL script that, when subsequently executed, will perform the backup of the database. Since the backup script is built from the current database structure, all of the existing database files will be automatically included in the backup. This ensures that no files are accidentally skipped, thereby invalidating the backup. If you are performing a disk-to-disk backup, a restore file will also be created to aid in restoring one or more of the database files to their original location.

12. If the database is running in ARCHIVELOG mode, execute the *crearch* script to create a variable containing the archive log destination (so that any archive log files can be included in the backup).

13. Execute the *ccontrol* script to create a script that, when executed, will recreate the control file for the database. This file will be included in the backup for an extra level of security, as well as providing a way to document all files and their locations.

14. If Oracle Applications are installed, execute the *dbousers* script to display a list of the current users (if any) in the database. This script calls the *allmemry* script to display the memory utilization before the concurrent manager pro-

cesses are shut down, and calls the *stopmgr* script to shut down the concurrent manager processes.

15. Execute the *allmemry* script to display the memory utilization statistics before the Oracle database is shut down.

16. Execute the *dbousers* script to display a list of the current users (if any) in the database, prior to it being shut down, for debugging purposes. UNIX processes connected to the database are also displayed.

17. If Oracle Applications are installed, execute the *killunix* script in order to attempt to kill the UNIX processes for any leftover concurrent manager jobs that may not have properly shut down.

18. Execute the *dbousers* script again to display (for debugging purposes) a list of the current users (if any) that might still be connected to the database after the concurrent manager processes are killed.

19. Display a list of all database background processes and a list of the shared memory segments (for debugging purposes).

20. Execute the *dbostop* script to shut down the Oracle database. A list of any remaining UNIX processes that might be connected to the Oracle database is displayed for debugging purposes.

21. If Oracle Applications are installed, rename the standard concurrent manager log file to a filename ending in the 3-letter day of the week. This prevents the log file from continuously growing (eventually filling up the filesystem), keeps the last seven days of log files accessible on disk at all times for perusal, and automatically purges old log data (since every new file replaces the corresponding file that was created seven days ago).

22. Display memory utilization statistics before the actual backup script executes, for debugging purposes.

23. Execute the *backcln* script to remove any old backup files from their backup directories.

24. Execute the backup script created in step 11 to perform the backup of the database files to disk.

25. Display a list of all of the files that were actually backed up (for debugging purposes).

26. If the database is running in ARCHIVELOG mode, execute the *backarch* script to back up any archive logs that might exist for the database as follows:

    — Call the *copy_log* script to copy the archive logs and the current control files to the desired backup filesystem.

— Call the *delarch* script to delete all of the existing archive logs (since they are not needed anymore, now that the entire database has been successfully backed up). Because an active database can create one gigabyte or more of archive logs in a single day, it is important to routinely clean out the obsolete archive log files; the database will halt if the archive log file destination runs out of space.

27. If a full database export is specified (on the command line) take the following action:

   — Call the *dbostart* script to start the database in exclusive mode.

   — Delete any previously existing export dump files.

   — Execute the Oracle *exp* (Export) utility to perform a full export of the database to the desired disk filesystem.

   — Display a directory listing of the export dump file.

   — Compress the export dump file using the UNIX *compress* command to conserve disk and/or tape space.

   — Display a directory listing of the compressed export dump file.

28. Display a list of any database processes (for debugging).

29. Execute the *dbostop* script to shut down the database.

30. Execute the *dbostart* script to start the database normally and clear the previously-set "offline" flag.

31. Execute the *allmemry* script to display the memory utilization statistics after the Oracle database is started.

32. If you are running Oracle Applications, execute the *startmgr* script to start the standard concurrent manager process.

33. Display the ending time and then exit.

Hot Backup to a System Tape Device

1. Verify that the required script parameters are present.

2. Ensure that the ORACLE_SID is in the proper case.

3. Parse the command input line for optional parameter(s).

4. Check for the "offline" flag (which will cause the backup for this database to be skipped). This is an easy way for the DBA to skip the backup for a specific database. The *offline* script sets the flag, while the *online* script clears the flag.

5. Verify the ORACLE_SID value against a list of all valid database SID values.

6. Execute the *define* script to define the ORACLE_BASE, ORACLE_HOME, ENVNAME, USERNAME, and APPL_TOP values, which are associated with the ORACLE_SID. (The ENVNAME, USERNAME, and APPL_TOP environment variables are used when the database is used with Oracle Financial Applications. ENVNAME is the name of the application environment file, USERNAME is the username to use when executing Applications Object Library (AOL) calls for the database, and APPL_TOP is the application top directory associated with the specified database. These values are not used if Oracle applications are not installed.) The *define* script calls *replpath* to ensure that one (and only one) ORACLE_HOME is present in the PATH.

7. Set the "offline" flag if a cold backup is being performed. (The existence of this flag can be used by other cooperating scripts to determine whether to allow other applications or scripts access to the database.) The included *menu* script is an example of a script that presents a menu of all available databases to a user; a database that is being backed up will remove itself from the menu (by setting the "offline" flag before the backup and clearing the "offline" flag after the backup is complete).

8. If you are running Oracle Applications, display a list of any running concurrent manager processes (for debugging purposes).

9. Execute the *dbo_stat* script to determine whether the specified database is currently open. If the database is not running, call the *dbostart* script to start up and open the database. (This is so that SQL can be used to build a backup script).

10. Execute the *creback* script to build a SQL script that, when subsequently executed, will perform the backup of the database. Since the backup script is built from the current database structure, all of the existing database files will be automatically included in the backup, ensuring that no files are accidentally skipped, thereby invalidating the backup. If you are performing a disk-to-disk backup, a restore file will also be created, to aid in restoring one or more of the database files to their original location.

11. Execute the *crearch* script to create a variable containing the archive log destination (so that any archive log files can be included in the backup).

12. Execute the *ccontrol* script to create a script that, when executed, will recreate the control file for the database. This file will be included in the backup to provide an extra level of security, as well as to document all files and their locations.

13. Execute the *allmemry* script to display the memory utilization statistics before the Oracle database is shut down.

14. Display a list of all database background processes and a list of the shared memory segments (for debugging purposes).

15. Display memory utilization statistics before the actual backup script executes, for debugging purposes.

16. Execute the backup script created in step 10 to back up the database files to tape.

17. Execute the *backarch* script to back up any archive logs that might exist for the database.

18. Execute the *creback* script to create a SQL script that will switch redo log files and wait for the current log file to be archived.

19. *creback* is called to create a SQL script that will switch redo log files and then wait for the current log file to be archived. The wait is very important since the redo log files are not backed up during a hot backup, and this wait ensures that all database transactions in the redo log file are copied to the archived log files, which are backed up.

20. Execute the *copy_log* script to copy the archive logs and the current control files to the desired backup filesystem or tape.

21. Call the *delarch* script to delete all of the existing archive logs (since they are not needed anymore, now that the entire database has been successfully backed up). Note that because an active database can create one gigabyte or more of archive logs in a single day, it is important that obsolete archive log files be routinely cleaned out; the database will halt if the archive log file destination runs out of space.

22. If a full database export is specified on the command line, execute the Oracle *exp* (Export) utility to perform a full export of the database to the desired tape device.

23. Display a list of any database processes (for debugging).

24. Execute the *allmemry* script to display the memory utilization statistics after the Oracle database is started.

25. Display the ending time and then exit.

Hot Backup to Disk

1. Verify that the required script parameters are present.

2. Ensure that the ORACLE_SID is in the proper case.

3. Parse the command input line for optional parameter(s).

4. Check for the "offline" flag (which will cause the backup for this database to be skipped). This is an easy way for the DBA to skip the backup for a spe-

cific database. The *offline* script sets the flag, while the *online* script clears the flag.

5. Verify the ORACLE_SID value against a list of all valid database SID values.

6. Execute the *define* script to define the ORACLE_BASE, ORACLE_HOME, ENVNAME, USERNAME, and APPL_TOP values, which are associated with the ORACLE_SID. (The ENVNAME, USERNAME, and APPL_TOP environment variables are used when the database is used with Oracle Financial Applications. ENVNAME is the name of the application environment file, USERNAME is the username to use when executing Applications Object Library (AOL) calls for the database, and APPL_TOP is the application top directory associated with the specified database. These values are not used if Oracle applications are not installed.) The *define* script calls *replpath* to ensure that one (and only one) ORACLE_HOME is present in the PATH.

7. Set the "offline" flag if a cold backup is being performed. (The existence of this flag can be used by other cooperating scripts to determine whether to allow other applications or scripts access to the database.) The included *menu* script is an example of a script that presents a menu of all available databases to a user; a database that is being backed up will remove itself from the menu (by setting the "offline" flag before the backup and clearing the "offline" flag after the backup is complete).

8. Execute the *calcbkup* script to calculate the desired file system that will contain the database backup files.

9. Execute the *dbo_stat* script to determine whether the specified database is currently open. If the database is not running, call the *dbostart* script to start up and open the database. (This is so that SQL can be used to build a backup script).

10. Execute the *creback* script to build a SQL script that, when subsequently executed, will perform the backup of the database. Since the backup script is built from the current database structure, all of the existing database files will be automatically included in the backup, ensuring that no files are accidentally skipped, thereby invalidating the backup. If you are performing a disk-to-disk backup, a restore file will also be created to aid in restoring one or more of the database files to their original location.

11. Execute the *ccontrol* script to create a script that, when executed, will recreate the control file for the database. This file will be included in the backup to provide an extra level of security, as well as to document all files and their locations.

12. Execute the *allmemry* script to display the memory utilization statistics before the Oracle database is shut down.

13. Execute the *dbousers* script to display a list of the current users (if any) in the database prior to its being shut down, for debugging purposes. UNIX processes connected to the database are also displayed.

14. Execute the *backcln* script to remove any old backup files from their backup directories.

15. Execute the backup script created in step 10 to back up the database files to disk.

16. Display a list of all of the files that were actually backed up (for debugging purposes).

17. Execute the *backarch* script to back up any archive logs that might exist for the database.

18. Execute the *creback* script to create a SQL script that will switch redo log files and wait for the current log file to be archived.

19. *creback* is called to create a SQL script that will switch redo log files and then wait for the current log file to be archived. The wait is very important since the redo log files are not backed up during a hot backup, and this wait ensures that all database transactions in the redo log file are copied to the archived log files, which are backed up.

20. Execute the *copy_log* script to copy the archive logs and the current control files to the desired backup filesystem or tape.

21. Call the *delarch* script to delete all of the existing archive logs (since they are not needed anymore, now that the entire database has been successfully backed up). Note that since an active database can create one gigabyte or more of archive logs in a single day, it is important that obsolete archive log files be routinely cleaned out; the database will halt if the archive log file destination runs out of space.

22. If a full database export is specified on the command line, take the following action:

    — Delete any previously existing export dump file.

    — Execute the Oracle *exp* (Export) utility to perform a full export of the database to the desired disk filesystem or tape device.

    — Display a directory listing of the export dump file.

    — Compress the export dump file using the UNIX *compress* command in order to conserve disk and/or tape space.

    — Display a directory listing of the compressed export dump file.

23. Execute the *allmemry* script to display the memory utilization statistics after the Oracle database is started.

24. Display the ending time and then exit.

Hot Backup to Third-Party Device

1. Verify that the required script parameters are present.

2. Ensure that the ORACLE_SID is in the proper case.

3. Parse the command input line for optional parameter(s).

4. Check for the "offline" flag (which will cause the backup for this database to be skipped). This is an easy way for the DBA to skip the backup for a specific database. The *offline* script sets the flag, while the *online* script clears the flag.

5. Verify the ORACLE_SID value against a list of all valid database SID values.

6. Execute the *define* script to define the ORACLE_BASE, ORACLE_HOME, ENVNAME, USERNAME, and APPL_TOP values, which are associated with the ORACLE_SID. (The ENVNAME, USERNAME, and APPL_TOP environment variables are used when the database is used with Oracle Financial Applications. ENVNAME is the name of the application environment file, USERNAME is the username to use when executing Applications Object Library (AOL) calls for the database, and APPL_TOP is the application top directory associated with the specified database. These values are not used if Oracle applications are not installed.) The *define* script calls *replpath* to ensure that one (and only one) ORACLE_HOME is present in the PATH.

7. Set the "offline" flag if a cold backup is being performed. (The existence of this flag can be used by other cooperating scripts to determine whether to allow other applications or scripts access to the database.) The included *menu* script is an example of a script that presents a menu of all available databases to a user; a database that is being backed up will remove itself from the menu (by setting the "offline" flag before the backup and clearing the "offline" flag after the backup is complete).

8. Execute the *dbo_stat* script to determine whether the specified database is currently open. If the database is not running, call the *dbostart* script to start up and open the database. (This is so that SQL can be used to build a backup script).

9. Execute the *creback* script to build a SQL script that, when subsequently executed, will perform the backup of the database. Since the backup script is built from the current database structure, all of the existing database files will be automatically included in the backup, ensuring that no files are accidentally skipped, and thereby invalidating the backup. If you are performing a

disk-to-disk backup, a restore file will also be created to aid in restoring one or more of the database files to their original location.

10. Execute the *crearch* script to create a variable containing the archive log destination (so that any archive log files can be included in the backup).

11. Execute the *ccontrol* script to create a script that, when executed, will recreate the control file for the database. This file will be included in the backup to provide an extra level of security, as well as to document all files and their locations.

12. Execute the *allmemry* script to display the memory utilization statistics before the Oracle database is shut down.

13. Execute the *dbousers* script to display a list of the current users (if any) in the database prior to its being shut down, for debugging purposes. UNIX processes connected to the database are also displayed.

14. Execute the *backup* script created in step 9 to alter the tablespaces to BEGIN BACKUP mode and to then pass the file names of the database files to the *copy_log* script. The *copy_log* script may need to be modified in order to interface with your third-party vendor's backup product (see the *copy_log* script description for details).

15. Execute the *copy_log* script to start the backup of the previously-passed list of database files; *copy_log* will wait until the third-party backup process has completed.

16. Execute the *creback* script to create a SQL script that will be executed in order to alter the tablespaces to END BACKUP mode.

17. Execute the SQL script created in step 16 to perform the actual ALTER TABLESPACE END BACKUP command for each tablespace.

18. Execute the *backarch* script to back up any archive logs that might exist for the database.

19. Execute the *copy_log* script to initialize the list of control files and archive logs that are to be backed up.

20. Execute the *creback* script to create a SQL script that will switch redo log files and then wait for the current log file to be archived.

21. Execute the SQL script created in step 20 to perform the actual switching of the redo logs, and wait for the current log to be archived.

22. Execute the *copy_log* script to start the backup of the previously passed list of archive logs and control files.

23. Call the *delarch* script to delete all of the existing archive logs (since they are not needed anymore, now that the entire database has been successfully

backed up). Note that since an active database can create one gigabyte or more of archive logs in a single day, it is important that obsolete archive log files be routinely cleaned out; the database will halt if the archive log file destination runs out of space.

24. If a full database export is specified on the command line, execute the Oracle *exp* (Export) utility to perform a full export of the database.

25. Display a list of any database processes (for debugging).

26. Execute the *allmemry* script to display the memory utilization statistics after the Oracle database is started.

27. Display the ending time and then exit.

Backup Script and File Descriptions

This section contains the descriptions of all of the backup scripts.

archwait.sql

Directory: *$DBA*
File Type: SQL Script
Edit Required: No
Output File: No

This script is called by the hot backup script created by the *creback* script. The purpose of this script is to wait for all online redo logs that need archiving to be copied to the archive destination by the ARCH process.

backPROD

Directory: *$DBA*
File Type: Shell Script
Edit Required: Yes
Output File: No

This is an example batch script used to perform a backup for a specified (*<sid>*) database; in this case, *<sid>* is PROD.

This script is usually executed nightly by a *cron* job that, in turn, executes the *$DBA/backup* script. Since this file is a sample, it must be edited to include all of *backup* parameters that pertain to the database that is being backed up; see the *$DBA/backup* script for parameter information.

The *back<sid>* script usually performs the following steps:

1. Shuts down SQL*Net (optionally).

2. Performs a backup of the *<sid>* database.

3. Restarts SQL*Net (optionally).

NOTE	This script must be manually edited to indicate your desired backup options. (The backup options are described in the *backup* script.)

This script is usually executed by *crontab*. It executes the *backup, startnet,* and *stopnet* scripts.

backPROD.dat

Directory: *$DBA*
File Type: Data File
Edit Required: Yes
Output File: No

This script is an example backup override data file that you can use when the total size of all files being backed up exceeds the maximum size allowed in a single UNIX filesystem. (See the "Installation and Configuration Instructions" early in this chapter for details regarding the backup utilities.) Note that the export dump file (if a full export is being performed as part of the backup processing) will be created on the first filesystem listed in this file.

backarch

Directory: *$DBA*
File Type: Shell Script
Edit Required: No
Output File: No

This script is called by the *backup* script to back up any archived redo log files for a given database. After backing up the archived redo log files, it then calls the *$DBA/delarch* script to delete any obsolete archived redo log files, since they are no longer needed. Along with the archive log backup, this script will also back up any control file recreation scripts and database restore scripts that exist. (See the *backup* script for details.)

backcln

Directory: *$DBA*
File Type: Shell Script
Edit Required: No
Output File: No

This script is called by the *backup* script to delete all old files from the filesystem(s) containing the backup files for a given database.

backdisp

Directory: *$DBA*
File Type: Shell Script
Edit Required: No
Output File: No

This script is called by the *backup* script to display a list of the files that were backed up for a given database, so that they will appear in the batch job log file.

backup

Directory: *$DBA*
File Type: Shell Script
Edit Required: No
Output File: No

This is the main backup script. It performs the desired (cold or hot) backup of the specified ($1) database. It can perform the backup from filesystems or raw device partitions, to disk or tape, directly or using UNIX third-party backup utilities.

This script optionally performs a full database export. Any Oracle Applications *std* internal concurrent manager log file is automatically renamed, if it exists. If the database files are contained in UNIX filesystems, the *backup* script will create two additional scripts, which will be included in the backup. The first is a script that can be used to recreate the database's control file. (It can also be used to document the database data file locations.) The second is a script that, when executed, restores the existing database files from the backup filesystems. (It can be easily edited to restore only the file(s) that were lost or corrupted.)

The many different backup script options available are normally controlled by command line parameters; see the comments in the script for further information. This script is normally executed by the *back*<sid> shell script (which itself is usually scheduled as a cron job.) The backup script executes the *allmemry, backarch, backcln, backdisp, calcbkup, ccontrol, crearch, creback, dbo_stat, dbo_stop, dbostart, dbousers, define, fixcase, killunix, mailto, offline, online, startmgr, stop-mgr,* and *valid_db* scripts (along with many of the commonly executed scripts.)

calcbkup

Directory: *$DBA*
File Type: Shell Script
Edit Required: No
Output File: No

This script is executed by the backup script to calculate (and print) the backup filesystem for the specified $ORACLE_SID database. If there is an override file, then the *first* file system listed in it will be printed. (This is the filesystem that will also contain the export dump file, if a full database export was specified to be performed as part of the backup processing.)

ccontrol

Directory: *$DBA*
File Type: Shell Script
Edit Required: No
Output File: *cr_<sid>.sql*

The *ccontrol* script is called by the backup script to create a SQL script file, which can then be used to recreate a control file for a database. It can also be executed independently of the backup process, whenever you want to create a script to recreate a control file. This script executes the *ccontrol.sql* script.

```
The following is an example of a file that ccontrol will create:
create controlfile set database PROD logfile
group 1 ('/u10/oracle/oradata/PROD/data/redo1',
        '/u12/oracle/oradata/PROD/data/redo1') size 10240K,
group 2 ('/u10/oracle/oradata/PROD/data/redo2',
        '/u12/oracle/oradata/PROD/data/redo2') size 10240K,
group 3 ('/u10/oracle/oradata/PROD/data/redo3',
        '/u12/oracle/oradata/PROD/data/redo3') size 10240K,
group 4 ('/u10/oracle/oradata/PROD/data/redo4',
        '/u12/oracle/oradata/PROD/data/redo4') size 10240K,
group 5 ('/u10/oracle/oradata/PROD/data/redo5',
        '/u12/oracle/oradata/PROD/data/redo5') size 10240K
resetlogs
NOARCHIVELOG
MAXDATAFILES 1022
MAXLOGFILES 64
MAXLOGMEMBERS 5
MAXINSTANCES 10
MAXLOGHISTORY 1000
 datafile '/u08/oracle/oradata/PROD/data/system.dbf' size 102400K
```

```
, '/u18/oracle/oradata/PROD/data/rollback_01' size 1254400K
, '/u19/oracle/oradata/PROD/data/temp_01' size 1484800K
, '/u10/oracle/oradata/PROD/data/tools_01' size 20480K
, '/u13/oracle/oradata/PROD/data/users_01' size 61440K
, '/u04/oracle/oradata/PROD/data/subscriber_01' size 358400K
, '/u07/oracle/oradata/PROD/data/subscriber_ndx_01' size 358400K
, '/u06/oracle/oradata/PROD/data/activity_01' size 460800K
, '/u16/oracle/oradata/PROD/data/activity_ndx_01' size 307200K
, '/u12/oracle/oradata/PROD/data/area_01' size 1024K
, '/u10/oracle/oradata/PROD/data/area_ndx_01' size 1024K
, '/u12/oracle/oradata/PROD/data/cutoff_01' size 2048K
, '/u04/oracle/oradata/PROD/data/cutoff_ndx_01' size 2048K
, '/u12/oracle/oradata/PROD/data/product_01' size 1024K
, '/u10/oracle/oradata/PROD/data/product_ndx_01' size 1024K
, '/u12/oracle/oradata/PROD/data/day_01' size 2048K
, '/u10/oracle/oradata/PROD/data/day_ndx_01' size 6144K
```

ccontrol.sql

Directory: *$DBA*
File Type: SQL Script
Edit Required: No
Output File: *cr_<sid>.sql*

This SQL script is called by the *ccontrol* script. It creates a temporary table that is used to create the control file script.

cr_alex

Directory: *$DBA*
File Type: Shell Script
Edit Required: Optional
Output File: Specified *opcard* File
Syntax: `cr_alex opcard`

opcard
    Name of the opcard file; this file may exist or will be created.

This script creates the Alexandria Backup opcard whose name is specified as the parameter to the script. Any existing opcard with the same name is replaced. This script can be used with the backup scripts to interface to a third-party backup product.

The *copy_log* script can be modified to call this *cr_alex* script in order to create an opcard to back up the specified database files.

crearch

Directory: *$DBA*
File Type: Shell Script
Edit Required: No
Output File: No

The *crearch* script defines the ARCHSTART and ARCHEND environment variables (containing the start and the end of the archive log file specification) for the specified database. This script is executed by the *backup* script.

creback

Directory: *$DBA*
File Type: Shell Script
Edit Required: No
Output File: *bkup*
Syntax: creback *sid*

sid
     The Oracle SID for the database to be backed up.

This script is executed by the *backup* script to create a shell script (*bkup*), which is subsequently executed in order to back up the files comprising the specified ($1) database. The files are backed up to a filesystem called */backup_sid* (where *sid* is the Oracle SID of the database being backed up.) If filesystem data files are being backed up to another disk filesystem, it will also create a script (*restore_<sid>*) that can be used to restore this database's files from the backup directory.

This script executes the *archwait.sql, creback.sql, fix_bkup,* and *fix_rest* scripts.

creback.sql

Directory: *$DBA*
File Type: SQL Script
Edit Required: No
Output File: *bkup_<sid>.lst*

This SQL script is called by *creback*. It creates a temporary table that in turn is used to create the UNIX shell script to perform the actual database backup.

delarch

Directory: *$DBA*
File Type: Shell Script
Edit Required: No
Output File: No

The *delarch* script is called by the *backarch* script to delete any obsolete archived redo log files for a given database. This script calls the *$DBA/delarch2* script to delete each individual archived redo log file.

delarch2

Directory: *$DBA*
File Type: Shell Script
Edit Required: No
Output File: No

The *delarch2* script is called by the *delarch* script to delete an individual archived redo log file for a given database, as described in the previous section.

fix_bkup

Directory: *$DBA*
File Type: Shell Script
Edit Required: No
Output File: No

This script is called by the *creback* script to fix the backup file system destinations for databases that have a backup override data file (*$DBA/back<sid>.dat*).

fix_rest

Directory: *$DBA*
File Type: Shell Script
Edit Required: No
Output File: No

This script is called by the *creback* script to fix the backup file system destinations for databases that have a backup override data file (*$DBA/back<sid>.dat*).

7

Oracle Applications Utilities

Oracle's suites of applications, such as Oracle Financials, Oracle Manufacturing, and so on—known collectively as Oracle Applications—are among the most popular in the world today. The databases serving these applications are critical to the success of the companies using them, and responsibility for efficient operation falls squarely on the DBA. Not only do you need to bring all of your traditional database administration skills (and accompanying scripts) to bear on these databases, but there are more "Applications-specific" issues to deal with as well. For example, for sites using Oracle Applications, you will need to be able to easily start, stop, or inquire of the status of the concurrent manager processes.

The scripts described in this chapter return the status of the concurrent manager process, and start or stop the concurrent managers for a given database. They have already been integrated with a number of the scripts discussed in the previous chapters, and are available for standalone use as well.

is_mgr

Directory: *$DBA*
File Type: Shell Script
Edit Required: No
Output File: Screen
Syntax: is_mgr *sid*

sid

> The Oracle SID for the database to be checked for the concurrent manager status.

This script returns the started/stopped status of the concurrent manager for the specified database. Values are returned as follows:

- A value of 0 is returned if the concurrent manager is not running.

- A value of 1 is returned if the concurrent manager is currently running.

- A value of 2 is returned if concurrent managers are not allowed for the database.

The *chkcm.sql* script is executed to obtain this information. The *is_mgr* script is executed by the *backup, startm, stat,* and *stopm* scripts.

Restrictions

- The USRNAME environment variable must contain the FND application username.

- The PWAPPLSYS environment variable must contain the FND application password.

- The PS_OPTS environment variable must contain the platform-specific *ps* utility option (normally set by the *$HOME/dbabatch* script.)

chkcm.sql

Directory: *$DBA*
File Type: SQL Script
Edit Required: No
Output File: Screen

This script is called by the *is_mgr* script to check the run status of the concurrent manager.

startm

Directory: *$DBA*
File Type: Shell Script
Edit Required: No
Output File: Screen
Syntax: startm *sid [diag]*

sid

> The Oracle SID of the database for which the concurrent manager is to be started.

diag

> If specified, will cause "diag=Y" to be appended to the concurrent manager startup command.

This script is used to start the concurrent manager for the specified database. No error is returned if the concurrent managers have already been started.

NOTE   This script needs read/write access to the *$FND_TOP/$1_log* directory and its data files in order for it to be executed by "oracle" (since those directories are normally owned by the application owner). This can be done by changing the group access for this directory and its files to allow read/write access, and by granting that group to "oracle" (so that "oracle" uses the group access part of the file protection to gain access to this directory.)

The diag=Y specification can be appended to the concurrent manager startup command for use in diagnosing operational problems.

The *is_mgr* script is called from the *startm* script to see if the concurrent managers are currently executing.

stopm

Directory: *$DBA*
File Type: Shell Script
Edit Required: No
Output File: Screen
Syntax: `startm sid`

sid
    The Oracle SID of the database for which the concurrent manager is to be stopped.

This script is used to stop the concurrent manager for the specified database. No error will occur if the concurrent managers are already shut down.

The *is_mgr* script is called from the *stopm* script to see if the concurrent managers are currently executing.

NOTE   You can change the DEACTIVATE status to ABORT to cause the concurrent managers to immediately shut down (aborting any running batch jobs), instead of waiting in the normal way for batch jobs to finish.

III

Scripts for Developers and Designers

This part of the book contains scripts that will be useful to those who are designing and developing Oracle databases and application programs, as well as to the DBAs who must support these systems.

8

Database-Design/ DDL Utilities

The scripts described in this chapter allow DBAs and developers to easily create, analyze, report, or reverse-engineer any of the objects in the database.

Good practice dictates that the DBA and/or the developer of an Oracle system should always have scripts that can recreate all of the objects in the database. This is especially useful when global edits need to be performed on various objects, when documenting the objects within a database, and when creating a backup of the object definitions for use when they need to be recreated.

In the real world, objects are often created "on the fly" using interactive SQL. In some cases, the scripts to create objects are lost or do not properly represent the current structure of an Oracle object. For example, a table might be initially created, but later a column definition is modified or new columns are added. Even if the original object creation scripts are unavailable, or are out of date, the creation scripts can easily be recreated from the data dictionary by using the scripts we've included in this chapter.

Other scripts provided here allow the DBA or developer to easily and quickly view or modify all of the interrelationships between tables, indexes, and constraints, without having to understand the underlying data dictionary structures or needing to write SQL code.

analinds.sql

Directory: *$DBA*
File Type: SQL Script
Edit Required: Optional
Output File: *analinds.lis*

This script determines the appropriateness of all indexes on all tables, except those owned by SYS and SYSTEM (although you can easily edit the script to analyze only specific indexes for specific tables). It does this by calculating the cardinality (that is, the percentage of all rows that are returned when querying for a specific indexed key) of all columns comprising each index on each table. This script does *not* execute the ANALYZE statement, so cost-based optimization will not be automatically enabled when this script is executed. This script creates an analysis report (*analinds.lis*) listing all of the analyzed tables and indexes.

Sample report

```
       Distinct
Object Owner / Name                       Num Rows     Keys      Keys  Cardinality
-------------------------------------   -------------  --------  --------- ------------
OPS$ORACLE.CUTOFF                             60708
Unique IND_CUTOFF_01                                   60630     99.872%      .00165%
             Indexed columns: DAY1, DAY2
       Bitmap IND_CUTOFF_02                                12      .020%      8.33333%
             Indexed columns: CUTOFF_MONTH
       Bitmap IND_CUTOFF_03                                 4      .007%     25.00000%
             Indexed columns: CUTOFF_QUARTER
       Bitmap IND_CUTOFF_04                                 1      .002%    100.00000%
             Indexed columns: CUTOFF_YEAR
```

This report shows the table and the number of rows in the table. For each index that exists for the table, it shows:

- The number of rows having distinct keys

- The percentage of distinct keys to the total number of rows in the table

- The cardinality of the columns

The report allows the DBA to easily locate inappropriately-indexed columns in the tables. Non-bitmap indexes having a high cardinality, or bitmap indexes having a low cardinality, are automatically flagged on the report as possibly being inappropriate.

analyze.sql

Directory: *$DBA*
File Type: SQL Script
Edit Required: No
Output File: *analyze.lis*

This script performs an ANALYZE COMPUTE STATISTICS on all tables and indexes not owned by SYS. It creates an analysis report (*analyze.lis*), describing all of the tables and indexes that were analyzed. Non-bitmap indexes having a high cardinality, or bitmap indexes having a low cardinality, are automatically flagged on the report as possibly being inappropriate.

Restrictions

- This script may take many hours when analyzing large tables.

- ANALYZE will *automatically* turn on cost-based optimization.

- Oracle requires locks on the tables to be analyzed. If this requirement prevents this script from successfully executing, use the *analinds.sql* script, as previously described, to obtain most of the same functionality.

- The script uses the DBMS_DDL.ANALYZE_OBJECT built-in procedure. This procedure requires that the DBMS_DDL package be available and that EXECUTE access be provided to the DBA account.

avgrow.sql

Directory: *$DBA*
File Type: SQL Script
Edit Required: Yes
Output File: Screen

This is a template script that calculates the space of an average row and the number of rows, from the actual data stored in the database, for use when sizing tables and indexes. To use this script, you must add the name of the target table to the FROM clause.

bad_cons.sql

Directory: *$DBA*
File Type: SQL Script
Edit Required: No
Output File: *bad_cons.lis*

The *bad_cons.sql* script displays information about the constraints whose owner of the primary key constraint does not match the table's owner. With some Oracle versions, this condition can cause ORA-00600 errors with an argument of 12838 to appear in the trace dump files. Once the potential problems are identified by using this script, you can eliminate this error by disabling the constraint, and reenabling it while connecting as the table's owner.

cdindex

Directory: *$DBA*
File Type: Shell Script
Edit Required: No
Output File: *bad_cons.lis, <table_name>_drop.sql, <table_name>_create.sql*
Syntax: `cdindex schema table_name action`

schema
> The schema name containing the table on which to create or drop indexes.

table_name
> The (uppercase) name of the table on which to create or drop indexes.

action
> The action to be performed: either CREATE or DROP.

This script will create or drop all nonunique indexes on a given table. This is especially useful when a table is being heavily modified or loaded. All nonessential indexes (other than primary or unique keys that are used to enforce constraints) should be dropped prior to modifying or loading the table, and then recreated after the table's modification or load has completed. Doing this will improve performance, since dropping and recreating the nonessential indexes may be a significant performance improvement over leaving them in place and having Oracle maintain those indexes for every row that is modified or loaded.

To execute the *cdindex* script, you must specify all three parameters listed here.

Processing flow

1. The script ensures that the ORACLE_SID environment variable has been set.

2. It ensures that the schema, table name, and action parameters have been specified.

3. If the action is DROP:

   — The script ensures that there is no *<table_name>_drop.sql* file in the current directory; the existence of this file indicates that the indexes for the given table have already been dropped.

   — It removes any *<table_name>_create.sql* file that might exist in the current directory.

   — It executes the *cindex.sql* file, which reads the data dictionary for the specified table name, and creates two output files: *<table_name>_drop.sql* (which, when executed, runs the SQL statements to drop all of the nonunique indexes on the given table) and *<table_name>_create.sql* (which, when executed, runs the SQL statements to create all of the nonunique indexes on the given table).

— It then executes the *<table_name>_drop.sql* file to perform the actual dropping of the nonunique indexes.

4. If the action is CREATE:

— The script ensures that there is an existing *<table_name>_drop.sql* file in the current directory; the existence of this file indicates that the indexes for the given table have already been dropped.

— It ensures that there is an existing *<table_name>_create.sql* file in the current directory; the existence of this file indicates that the indexes for the given table have not already been recreated.

— It executes the *<table_name>_create.sql* file to recreate the previously dropped indexes.

— It deletes the *<table_name>_drop.sql* and *<table_name>_create.sql* files.

Restrictions

- The ORACLE_SID and ORACLE_HOME environment variables must be set before executing the script.

- The *$DBA/cdindex.sql* file must exist (since that is the script that is called to create the index recreation script.)

- The OPS$username account must exist and it must have the required privileges to CREATE and DROP indexes on the specified table (as well as sufficient quotas.)

- The invoking user needs to have SELECT access to the SYS.DBA_INDEXES and SYS.DBA_IND_COLUMNS views.

cdindex.sql

Directory: *$DBA*
File Type: SQL Script
Edit Required: No
Output File: *table_drop.sql, table_create.sql*
Syntax: cdindex `schema` `table`

schema

The name of the schema (uppercase) containing the table specified.

table

The name of the table (uppercase) whose indexes are to be dropped or created.

This SQL script is called by the *cdindex* script to create the index recreation scripts, as described in the previous section.

chkcrdb

Directory: *$DBA*
File Type: Shell Script
Edit Required: No
Output File: Screen
Syntax: chkcrdb *[file]*

file
    The name of the output log file to be checked.

When an Oracle database is created, a very large log file (sometimes in excess of two megabytes) is created, containing a trace of all of the commands that were executed, along with all of the errors that were encountered during the database creation process.

The only way to ensure that the database creation was completely successful is to inspect the log file for any "ORA-" errors. Unfortunately, since most of the Oracle scripts first drop any existing objects prior to creating each object, there will be a very large number (more than 400 with Oracle 7.3!) of "ORA-01432: public synonym to be dropped does not exist" and "ORA-00942: table or view does not exist" error messages in the log file. You can safely ignore these errors if the object has never existed and is going to be created by the subsequent SQL statement. Since the log file is too large to manually inspect every error, most DBAs never bother to check this file for errors. This is unfortunate, since there may be a serious error, buried in the middle of the file, which may otherwise go undetected.

You can execute the *chkcrdb* shell script to display any unexpected errors in the specified database creation log file. The script can be executed any time after the database creation has been completed. The one optional argument allows you to specify the filename of the log file, but since it defaults to *$ORACLE_BASE/admin/$ORACLE_SID/create/crdb$ORACLE_SID.lst*, as long as you have properly defined the ORACLE_BASE and ORACLE_SID environment variables, you will normally never have to specify any argument to the script.

The script displays all "ORA-" errors in the log file, other than the ones that immediately follow a previous DROP *xxx* command. The result is usually a very small number of errors. Check them carefully!

chktable.sql

Directory: *$DBA*
Edit Required: No
Output File: Screen

This script checks a specific table's CHAR and VARCHAR2 columns for abnormal characters (e.g., quotes, apostrophes, or any control characters). When executed, it prompts for the table owner and name to be accessed. This script requires Oracle 7.2.2.3 (since dynamic SQL is used). The script will prompt for the name of the schema and table.

A maximum of ten CHAR and/or VARCHAR2 columns can be checked in a single table. (Use the *chktabl2.sql* script if you have more than ten columns.)

chktabl2.sql

Directory: *$DBA*
File Type: SQL Script
Edit Required: No
Output File: Screen

This script checks a specific table's CHAR and VARCHAR2 columns for abnormal characters (e.g., quotes, apostrophes, or any control characters). When executed, the script prompts for the table owner and name to be accessed. This script requires Oracle 7.2.2.3 (since dynamic SQL is used). The script will prompt for the name of the schema and table.

This script is similar to *chktable.sql*, but is used only when there are more than ten CHAR and/or VARCHAR2 columns in a table. (The *chktable.sql* script is limited to ten such columns.) This script is not as efficient as *chktable.sql*, since this script fetches all rows from the table for *each* CHAR and VARCHAR2 column in the table.

cindex

Directory: *$DBA*
File Type: Shell Script
Edit Required: Yes
Output File: *crindex.sql*

This script is used to create a SQL script containing DDL statements that creates a new index on a given table. It will automatically calculate the required INITIAL and NEXT extent values (saving the DBA lots of time and improving the reliability of the database).

The script performs the following steps:

1. It prompts for the ORACLE_SID of the database to be accessed and verifies it for accuracy.

2. It prompts for the name of the table on which the index is to be created. The *istable.sql* script is called to verify whether the table name matches an existing table in the specified database.

3. The *cindexd.sql* script is then called to create a menu listing of all of the columns in the specified table.

4. The script prompts for the column name to be included in the index. This step is repeated for every column that is to comprise the new index. (The user simply presses the <RETURN> key when no more columns are to be included in the index.)

5. The script prompts for the index name.

6. The *cindex.sql* script is then called to create the actual script (cr_index.sql) containing the DDL statement, which can be used to create the index.

7. The *trunc* script is executed to remove all trailing spaces from each line of the *cr_index.sql* file.

Note that one simple edit is required before running the *cr_index.sql* script: you must specify the name of the tablespace that is to contain the new index.

Restrictions

- The following script files must exist and be found in the PATH: *define, fix-case, trunc,* and *valid_db.*

- The following SQL script files must exist: *cindex.sql, cindexd.sql,* and *istable.sql.*

- *$TOOLS/getsyi, $TOOLS/replpath,* and *$TOOLS/database* must exist.

- If Oracle Applications are being used, *$APPL_TOP/$ENVNAME.env* must exist.

cindex.sql

Directory: *$DBA*
File Type: SQL Script
Edit Required: No
Output File: *cr_index.sql*

This script will create a SQL script that can be used to create a correctly sized index for the specified table. It is called by the *cindex* script.

cindexd.sql

Directory: *$DBA*
File Type: SQL Script
Edit Required: No
Output File: *cindexd.tmp*

This SQL script displays and creates a file containing the columns of a table. It is called by the *cindex* script.

crbodys.sql

Directory: *$DBA*
File Type: SQL Script
Edit Required: Optional
Output File: *crbody.sql*

This script creates a SQL script (*cr_body.sql*) that will contain all of the CREATE PACKAGE BODY statements for all package bodies in the database except those owned by SYS. Running this script allows the DBA to quickly and easily reverse-engineer the scripts to create all of the user-defined packages in the database.

The resulting script file is especially useful in the following cases:

- To create a backup copy of the existing object definitions. This does not preclude the use of a database export, since export will back up the data, as well as the object definitions. This script only creates the definition of the object.

- To duplicate the existing object definitions in another database (possibly on another system), since the resulting SQL script is completely portable.

- To document all of the existing objects in the database (even if the original object creation scripts were lost or are otherwise unavailable).

- To easily make mass changes to the objects. Suppose that you want to move all objects that are located in one tablespace to another. This is what you do:

    a. Simply edit the script to select only the objects in the original tablespace.

    b. Run this script, and then edit the output file, changing all of the tablespace names in one simple global edit from the old to the new tablespace.

    c. Drop all of the objects in the original tablespace.

    d. Finally, execute the newly revised script to create the object definitions in the new tablespace.

crclusts.sql

Directory: *$DBA*
File Type: SQL Script
Edit Required: Optional
Output File: *cr_clust.sql*

This script creates a SQL script that will contain all of the CREATE CLUSTER statements for all clusters in the database except those owned by SYS. (See the *crbodys.sql* script for further information.)

crcomms.sql

Directory: *$DBA*
File Type: SQL Script
Edit Required: No
Output File: *cr_comm.sql*

This script creates a SQL script that will contain all of the COMMENT ON statements for all comments in the database except those owned by SYS. (See the *crbodys.sql* script for further information.)

crconstr.sql

Directory: *$DBA*
File Type: SQL Script
Edit Required: No
Output File: *cr_const.sql*

This script creates a script that will contain all of the ALTER TABLE ADD CONSTRAINT statements for all constraints in the database except those owned by SYS. (See the *crbodys.sql* script for further information.)

crdb

Directory: *$DBA*

File Type: Shell Script

Edit Required: No

Output File: *cr<sid>.sql*

Syntax: crdb *[oracle_sid]* *['username/password']*

oracle_sid

Optional Oracle SID for which this script is being run (the default is the current ORACLE_SID).

username/password

Optional username and password to access the DBA_ and V$_ tables in order to create the script file. If the default ("/") account is selected by omitting the username/password, then an OPS$username account must exist in the specified database.

This script creates a script (*cr<SID>.sql*) to recreate a database's structure, with all of its tablespaces, data files, redo logs, and rollback segments. This script is especially useful in doing the following:

* Easily creating a database's structure

* Recreating a copy of the database (possibly on another node)

* Documenting the existing database's structure

When used in conjunction with a full export, this script can be used to easily back up and recreate the full database. However, it is important that the resulting script be used only after careful review since it is not possible to test such a script under every conceivable condition.

Here is an example of invoking this script:

```
crdb PROD 'system/manager'
```

Restrictions

* The ORACLE_BASE environment variable must be set. The *INIT.ORA* file for STARTUP is assumed to be in the *$ORACLE_BASE/admin/$ORACLE_SID/ init$ORACLE_SID_0.ora* file. A warning will be displayed if the PFILE clause on the STARTUP command needs to be manually changed.

* *oraenv* must be found in the PATH.

Sample output

```
rem  **********************************************

rem  *  Script    : crdbdev.sql to Create Database
```

```
rem  *   Date       : 10/27/97   08:10:05
rem  *   Notes :
rem  *   - This script includes CREATE DATABASE,
rem  *       CREATE other TABLESPACES, CREATE ROLLBACK
rem  *       SEGMENT, statements.
rem  *       It also runs catalog.sql, catproc.sql,
rem  *       dbmspool.sql, prvtpool.sql, and utlmontr.sql under SYS
rem  *       and catdbsyn.sql and pupbld.sql under SYSTEM
rem  *
rem  *   - You should (if needed) :
rem  *       point to the correct init.ora file,
rem  *       and ensure that the rollback segments are
rem  *       enabled in the init.ora file after the
rem  *       database is created.
rem  *
rem  *************************************************
rem
rem  Database name        : dev
rem  Database created     : 01/08/97 12:45:04
rem  Database log_mode    : NOARCHIVELOG
rem  Database blocksize   : 2048 bytes
rem  Database buffers     : 200 blocks
rem  Database log_buffers : 32768 blocks
rem  Database ifile       :
rem         /app/oracle/admin/dev/pfile/configdev.ora
rem
rem  Database Options     :
rem
rem  Note:  Use ALTER SYSTEM BACKUP CONTROLFILE TO TRACE;
rem         to generate a script to create controlfile
rem         and compare it with the output of this script.
rem         Add MAXLOGFILES, MAXDATAFILES, etc. if reqd.
rem
spool crdbdev.lst
connect internal
startup nomount pfile=/app/oracle/admin/dev/pfile/initdev_0.ora
/* please verify/change the following parameters as needed */
CREATE DATABASE "dev"
    NOARCHIVELOG
    /* using actual control file values */
    MAXLOGFILES         32
    MAXLOGMEMBERS       2
    MAXDATAFILES        30
    MAXINSTANCES        8
    MAXLOGHISTORY       800
    DATAFILE '/oradata/oradata/dev/system01.dbf' SIZE 73804K,
           '/oradata/oradata/dev/sys2' SIZE 50M,
           '/oradata/oradata/dev/system03.dbf' SIZE 75M
    LOGFILE
    GROUP  1 ('/oradata/oradata/dev/redodev01.log' ) SIZE 500K,
    GROUP  2 ('/oradata/oradata/dev/redodev02.log' ) SIZE 500K,
    GROUP  3 ('/oradata/oradata/dev/redodev03.log' ) SIZE 500K;
;
```

```
rem ----------------------------------------
rem
rem  Need a basic rollback segment before proceeding
rem
CREATE ROLLBACK SEGMENT r000 TABLESPACE SYSTEM
    storage (initial 500K next 500K minextents 2);
ALTER ROLLBACK SEGMENT r000 ONLINE;
commit;
rem ----------------------------------------
rem
rem Create DBA views
rem
@$ORACLE_HOME/rdbms/admin/catalog.sql
commit;
rem ----------------------------------------
rem
rem  Additional Tablespaces
rem
rem ----------------------------------------
rem
CREATE TABLESPACE BRBS DATAFILE
    '/oradata/oradata/dev/brbs01.dbf' SIZE 329862K,
    '/oradata/oradata/dev/brbs02.dbf' SIZE 100M default storage
    (initial 10K next 10K pctincrease 50 minextents 1 maxextents 121);
rem
rem ----------------------------------------
rem
CREATE TABLESPACE DBCARE DATAFILE
    '/oradata/oradata/dev/dbc01.dbf' SIZE 5M default storage
    (initial 30K next 30K pctincrease 0 minextents 1 maxextents 99);
rem
rem ----------------------------------------
rem
CREATE TABLESPACE DES2 DATAFILE
    '/oradata/oradata/dev/des2data.dbf' SIZE 20M,
    '/oradata/oradata/dev/des2_data2' SIZE 10M default storage
    (initial 100K next 100K pctincrease 5 minextents 1 maxextents 121);
rem
rem ----------------------------------------
rem
CREATE TABLESPACE DES2_I DATAFILE
    '/oradata/oradata/dev/des2indx.dbf' SIZE 10M,
    '/oradata/oradata/dev/des2idx2.dbf' SIZE 10M default storage
    (initial 100K next 100K pctincrease 5 minextents 1 maxextents 121);
rem
rem ----------------------------------------
rem
CREATE TABLESPACE RBS DATAFILE
    '/oradata/oradata/dev/rbs01.dbf' SIZE 118908K,
    '/oradata/oradata/dev/rbs02.dbf' SIZE 50M default storage
    (initial 128K next 128K pctincrease 0 minextents 2 maxextents 121);
rem
rem ----------------------------------------
rem
```

```
CREATE TABLESPACE TEMPORARY_DATA DATAFILE
    '/oradata/oradata/dev/tempdata.dbf' SIZE 221142K default storage
    (initial 100K next 100M pctincrease 50 minextents 1 maxextents 121);
rem
rem --------------------------------------
rem
CREATE TABLESPACE TOOLS DATAFILE
    '/oradata/oradata/dev/tools01.dbf' SIZE 15M default storage
    (initial 10K next 10K pctincrease 50 minextents 1 maxextents 121);
rem
rem --------------------------------------
rem
CREATE TABLESPACE USERS DATAFILE
    '/oradata/oradata/dev/users01.dbf' SIZE 496752K default storage
    (initial 10K next 100M pctincrease 50 minextents 1 maxextents 121);
rem
rem --------------------------------------
rem
CREATE TABLESPACE USER_DATA DATAFILE
    '/oradata/oradata/dev/userdata.dbf' SIZE 758044K,
    '/oradata/oradata/dev/userdata02.dbf' SIZE 753762K,
    '/oradata/oradata/dev/userdata03.dbf' SIZE 100M default storage
    (initial 10K next 10M pctincrease 0 minextents 1 maxextents 121);
rem
rem --------------------------------------
rem
rem  Create additional rollback segments in the rollback tablespace
rem
rem --------------------------------------
rem
CREATE ROLLBACK SEGMENT BRBS TABLESPACE BRBS STORAGE
    (initial 1M next 1M minextents 10 maxextents 121 optimal 10M);
CREATE ROLLBACK SEGMENT HUGE TABLESPACE BRBS STORAGE
    (initial 20M next 20M minextents 2 maxextents 121);
CREATE ROLLBACK SEGMENT R01 TABLESPACE RBS STORAGE
    (initial 500K next 500K minextents 4 maxextents 121 optimal 2M);
CREATE ROLLBACK SEGMENT R02 TABLESPACE RBS STORAGE
    (initial 500K next 500K minextents 4 maxextents 121 optimal 2M);
CREATE ROLLBACK SEGMENT R03 TABLESPACE RBS STORAGE
    (initial 500K next 500K minextents 4 maxextents 121 optimal 2M);
CREATE ROLLBACK SEGMENT R04 TABLESPACE RBS STORAGE
    (initial 500K next 500K minextents 4 maxextents 121 optimal 2M);
ALTER ROLLBACK SEGMENT BRBS ONLINE;
ALTER ROLLBACK SEGMENT R01 ONLINE;
ALTER ROLLBACK SEGMENT R02 ONLINE;
ALTER ROLLBACK SEGMENT R03 ONLINE;
ALTER ROLLBACK SEGMENT R04 ONLINE;
rem
rem  Take the initial rollback segment (r000) offline
rem
ALTER ROLLBACK SEGMENT r000 OFFLINE;
rem
rem --------------------------------------
rem
```

```
ALTER USER SYS TEMPORARY TABLESPACE TEMPORARY_DATA;
ALTER USER SYSTEM TEMPORARY TABLESPACE TEMPORARY_DATA DEFAULT TABLESPACE TOOLS;
rem
rem ----------------------------------------
rem
rem  Run other @$ORACLE_HOME/rdbms/admin required scripts
rem
commit;
rem
@$ORACLE_HOME/rdbms/admin/catproc.sql
rem @$ORACLE_HOME/rdbms/admin/catparr.sql
@$ORACLE_HOME/rdbms/admin/dbmspool.sql
@$ORACLE_HOME/rdbms/admin/prvtpool.sql
@$ORACLE_HOME/rdbms/admin/utlmontr.sql
rem
commit;
rem
connect system/manager
@$ORACLE_HOME/sqlplus/admin/pupbld.sql
@$ORACLE_HOME/rdbms/admin/catdbsyn.sql
commit;
spool off
exit
```

crfuncs.sql

Directory: *$DBA*
File Type: SQL Script
Edit Required: No
Output File: *cr_func.sql*

This script creates a SQL script that contains all of the CREATE FUNCTION statements for all functions in the database except those owned by SYS. (See the *crbodys.sql* script for further information.)

crgrants.sql

Directory: *$DBA*
File Type: SQL Script
Edit Required: No
Output File: *cr_grant.sql*

This script creates a SQL script that will contain all of the GRANT statements for all grants in the database (except for those granted by SYS). (See the *crbodys.sql* script for further information.)

crindexs.sql

Directory: *$DBA*
File Type: SQL Script
Edit Required: No
Output File: *cr_index.sql*

This script creates a SQL script that will contain all of the CREATE INDEX statements for all indexes in the database (except those owned by SYS).

crlinks.sql

Directory: *$DBA*
File Type: SQL Script
Edit Required: No
Output File: *cr_link.sql*

This script creates a SQL script that will contain all of the CREATE DATABASE LINK statements for database links in the database.

crpacks.sql

Directory: *$DBA*
File Type: SQL Script
Edit Required: No
Output File: *cr_pack.sql*

This script creates a script that will contain all of the CREATE PACKAGE statements for all packages in the database (except those owned by SYS). (See the *crbodys.sql* script for further information.)

crprocs.sql

Directory: *$DBA*
File Type: SQL Script
Edit Required: No
Output File: *cr_proc.sql*

This script creates a SQL script that will contain all of the CREATE PROCEDURE statements for all procedures in the database (except those owned by SYS).

crprofs.sql

Directory: *$DBA*
File Type: SQL Script
Edit Required: No
Output File: *cr_prof.sql*

This script creates a SQL script that will contain all of the CREATE PROFILE statements for all profiles in the database.

crroles.sql

Directory: *$DBA*
File Type: SQL Script
Edit Required: No
Output File: *cr_role.sql*

This script creates a SQL script that will contain all of the CREATE ROLE statements for all roles in the database.

crseqs.sql

Directory: *$DBA*
File Type: SQL Script
Edit Required: No
Output File: *cr_seq.sql*

This script creates a SQL script that will contain all of the CREATE SEQUENCE statements for all sequences in the database.

WARNING   Because this script does not create a START WITH clause, the resulting script may need to be edited with a desired starting value if you want continuity of generated sequence numbers.

---

crsnaps.sql

Directory: *$DBA*
File Type: SQL Script
Edit Required: No
Output File: *cr_snap.sql*

This script creates a SQL script that will contain all of the CREATE SNAPSHOT statements for all snapshots in the database (except those owned by SYS).

crsnlogs.sql

Directory: *$DBA*
File Type: SQL Script
Edit Required: No
Output File: *cr_snlog.sql*

This script creates a SQL script that will contain all of the CREATE SNAPSHOT LOGS statements for all snapshots in the database (except those owned by SYS).

crsyns.sql

Directory: *$DBA*
File Type: SQL Script
Edit Required: No
Output File: *cr_syn.sql*

This script creates a SQL script that will contain all of the CREATE SYNONYM statements for all synonyms in the database.

crtables.sql

Directory: *$DBA*
File Type: SQL Script
Edit Required: No
Output File: *cr_table.sql*

This script creates a script that will contain all of the CREATE TABLE statements for all tables in the database (except those owned by SYS).

crtrigs.sql

Directory: *$DBA*
File Type: SQL Script
Edit Required: No
Output File: *cr_trig.sql*

This script creates a SQL script that will contain all of the CREATE TRIGGER statements for all triggers in the database.

crusers.sql

Directory: *$DBA*
File Type: SQL Script
Edit Required: No
Output File: *cr_user.sql*

This script creates a SQL script that will contain all of the CREATE USER statements for all users in the database (except SYS). Note that the resulting script will recreate passwords, but the passwords will be stored in the *cr_user.sql* script in encrypted form and will therefore be unreadable. However, we recommend that, for security purposes, you carefully protect this output file.

crviews.sql

Directory: *$DBA*
File Type: SQL Script
Edit Required: No
Output File: *cr_view.sql*

This script creates a SQL script that will contain all of the CREATE VIEW statements for all views in the database (except those owned by SYS).

dbdelete

Directory: *$DBA*
File Type: SQL Script
Edit Required: No
Output File: No

This script deletes an entire Oracle database by deleting the database files, redo log files, and control files for the specified ORACLE_SID.

The script performs the following functions:

1. Shuts down any Oracle Applications (e.g., Financials) concurrent manager processes (if any) that are running for the specified database.

2. Executes the *dbdelete.sql* script to create the shell script that will be executed to actually delete the associated files for this database.

3. Executes *dbostop* to shut down the database.

4. Executes the script created by *dbo_delete.sql* to delete the database files at the operating system level. After deleting the database files, the script itself will be automatically deleted.

5. Creates a *$DBA/noconc.<SID>* flag file (marking this database's concurrent managers as being unavailable, since there is no longer an APPLSYS account for the database).

6. Displays a message indicating that the database has been successfully deleted.

dbo_sql.sql

Directory: *$TOOLS*
File Type: SQL Script
Edit Required: No
Output File: *dbo_sql.lis*

This script produces a report of the SQL statements being executed by all current users of the specified database. It may be useful to allow various non-DBA accounts (such as application developers) the ability to execute this script file so that they can diagnose problems in their SQL statements. This can be accomplished by doing the following:

1. Execute the *make_ops_user* script (which creates an OPS$username account for a given username).

2. Then execute the *grant_tools* script (which grants select access to the required V$ and DBA tables to the OPS$username account.) This presumes that your current username has the WITH GRANT OPTION on these privileges so that you can grant these privileges to someone else.)

Unlike the normal V$SQLAREA view, this script will display the *full text* of the SQL statement being executed. This is accomplished by creating a custom data dictionary view of the required tables. The *$DBA/dbosqli.sql* script must first be executed by SYS, in order to create the required data dictionary view. (This view, rather than V$SQLAREA, is used since the sql_text column of V$SQLAREA is only 1000 bytes long, and many SQL statements are much longer than that.)

Sample report

```
10/27/97              DBO_SQL - SQL Text for database DEV users

Oracle     O/S
User       Username SQL Text
------     -------- -----------------------------------------------------------
OPS$ORACLE oracle   select username, sid, piece, osuser, sql_text from dbo_sql_text
                    order by 1, 2, 3
```

ddl

Directory: *$DBA*
File Type: Shell Script
Edit Required: No
Output File: *ddl_drop.sql, ddl_create.sql*

The *ddl* script provides an easy-to-use interface that allows the DBA to create SQL scripts that drop and/or recreate tables, indexes, and/or referential integrity constraints for all tables dependent on a given table, or for a specific index or constraint.

Depending on the answers to the various prompts, one of the associated *ddl* scripts (*ddltbls.sql, ddlndxs.sql, ddlndxs2.sql, ddlcon.sql, ddlcons.sql,* and *ddlcons2.sql*) is executed.

The *ddl* script first prompts for the ORACLE_SID of the database to be accessed. After verifying the ORACLE_SID, it then prompts for the schema and table name to be processed. If a table name is entered, the *istable.sql* script is executed to verify that the table name is valid, and then prompts the user to determine whether a script should be created to take the following action:

- Recreate the table?
- Recreate any index(es) on the table?
- Recreate any referential integrity constraint(s) that are dependent on the table?
- Recreate any referential integrity constraint(s) on the table?

If no table name is entered, the script will prompt for the index name to be processed. If no index name is entered, the script will prompt for the constraint name to be processed. Finally if no constraint name is entered, the script will terminate since no object has been specified.

After the last prompt, the script will run and create two other scripts:

ddl_drop.sql
   Containing the DROP statements for the specified object(s).

ddl_create.sql
   Containing the CREATE statements for the specified object(s).

depend

Directory: *$DBA*
File Type: Shell Script
Edit Required: No
Output File: *depend.lst*

This script creates a report of all dependencies for a specific database. It calls the *depend.sql* script to create the report.

Sample report

```
DEPEND - Dependencies

Dependent                Dependent Object                Object
Name                     Time      Name                  Time
-----------------------  --------- ----------------------- ---------
USER_CLU_COLUMNS         08-JAN-97 TAB$                   08-JAN-97
DBA_CLU_COLUMNS          08-JAN-97 TAB$                   08-JAN-97
SYS_OBJECTS              31-JAN-97 TAB$                   08-JAN-97
USER_TABLES              31-JAN-97 TAB$                   08-JAN-97
ALL_TABLES               31-JAN-97 TAB$                   08-JAN-97
DBA_TABLES               31-JAN-97 TAB$                   08-JAN-97
TAB                      31-JAN-97 TAB$                   08-JAN-97
MDLIB                    21-APR-97 DBA_TABLES             31-JAN-97
MDGEN                    21-APR-97 DBA_TABLES             31-JAN-97
MDEXEC                   21-APR-97 DBA_TABLES             31-JAN-97
MD_NIP                   21-APR-97 DBA_TABLES             31-JAN-97
```

This report shows that the DBA_TABLES view is dependent on the TAB$ table, and the MDLIB view is dependent on the DBA_TABLES view.

depend.sql

Directory: *$DBA*
File Type: SQL Script
Edit Required: No
Output File: *depend.lst*

This script creates a file containing a list of all dependencies in the database.

descview.sql

Directory: *$DBA*
File Type: SQL Script
Edit Required: No
Output File: *descview.lis*

This script performs a DESCRIBE of each of the V$ and DBA_ views to a file, so that these can be compared to new Oracle versions to see what views are new or have been modified.

discon.sql

Directory: *$DBA*
File Type: SQL Script
Edit Required: No
Output File: *disconxx.sql*

This script disables all primary key, unique, and foreign key constraints for a database (except those owned by SYS). You'll find this script useful when you are trying to import multiple tables into a database. In many cases, you would receive an error when the imported rows violated integrity constraints. In such cases, do the following:

1. Execute this script (to disable the constraints on the desired table(s)).

2. Perform the import.

3. Execute the *enacon.sql* script to reenable the disabled constraints.

You can easily edit this script to disable all constraints for a specific table or schema.

drop_obj.sql

Directory: *$DBA*
File Type: SQL Script
Edit Required: No
Output File: No
Syntax: `drop_obj` *type name*

type
　　The type of object being dropped; may be TABLE or SYNONYM.

name
　　The name of the object being dropped.

This script drops the specified table or synonym object, if it exists. No drop is attempted if the object does not exist. This script can be used to avoid producing any error messages when a script needs to drop any existing object just prior to creating that object from scratch.

enacon.sql

Directory: *$DBA*
File Type: SQL Script
Edit Required: No
Output File: No

This script enables all primary key, unique, and foreign key constraints for a database (except those owned by SYS). This is most useful when you are trying to import multiple tables into a database. In many cases, you would receive an error when the imported rows violated integrity constraints. In that case, you should first execute the *discon.sql* script (to disable the constraints on the desired table(s)), perform the import, and then execute this script to reenable the disabled constraints. This script can be easily edited to enable all constraints for a specific table or schema.

file_use

Directory: *$DBA*
File Type: Shell Script
Edit Required: No
Output File: *file_use.lis*

This shell script lists all of the database tablespace and file specifications in a single comprehensive report, which allows the DBA to see easily all of the structures that comprise a given database. The report provides (usually on a single page per database) all of the following information about each database:

- Each tablespace, its associated data file(s), their sizes, and their status
- Each redo log file group, their members, their sizes, and their status
- Each control file name specification
- Any file name specification
- The archive log file specification and its status (enabled/disabled)
- The total number of megabytes for all of the preceding objects

If an ORACLE_SID is specified as a parameter to the script, a report will be created for only that specific ORACLE_SID. By default, a report will be created for all databases found in the *$TOOLS/database* file.

The script file will prompt for whether you want to translate any symbolic links to their actual directories. Why would you want to do this? Since many sites have their data file paths within the Oracle database all pointing to a set of symbolic links (usually in a single directory), the normal report would show all data files as existing in the same directory or mount point. This prompt allows you to have the script substitute the actual location of the data files in place of the referenced symbolic link. Note that if your site does not use symbolically linked data file specifications, you should respond to this prompt with an "N," so that processing time is not incurred for searching for nonexistent symbolic links.

Execute the *file_use.sql* script to obtain the information for the report.

Sample report

```
12/10/97                    FILE_USE - Files for database PROD
```

Type	Tablesp	File Name	Actual MB on Disk	Stat	Seq#	Arc
Data	AOL_DAT	/u07/oracle/data/PROD/aol_dat01.dbf	184	Avail		
Data	AOL_NDX	/u07/oracle/data/PROD/aol_ndx01.dbf	79	Avail		
Data	AP_DAT	/u14/oracle/data/PROD/ap_dat02.dbf	315	Avail		
Data		/u23/oracle/data/PROD/ap_dat01.dbf	393	Avail		
Data	AP_NDX	/u22/oracle/data/PROD/ap_ndx01.dbf	341	Avail		
Data	BRL	/u20/oracle/data/PROD/brl01.dbf	5	Avail		
Data	INV_DAT	/u07/oracle/data/PROD/inv_dat01.dbf	419	Avail		
Data	INV_NDX	/u07/oracle/data/PROD/inv_ndx01.dbf	524	Avail		
Data	NOETIX	/u10/oracle/data/PROD/noetix.dbf	26	Avail		
Data	PO_DAT	/u12/oracle/data/PROD/po_dat01.dbf	524	Avail		
Data		/u12/oracle/data/PROD/po_dat02.dbf	472	Avail		
Data	PO_NDX	/u14/oracle/data/PROD/po_ndx01.dbf	524	Avail		
Data		/u14/oracle/data/PROD/po_ndx02.dbf	551	Avail		
Data	RBS	/u11/oracle/data/PROD/rbs01.dbf	524	Avail		
Data		/u11/oracle/data/PROD/rbs02.dbf	315	Avail		
Data	SHR_DAT	/u21/oracle/data/PROD/shr_dat01.dbf	629	Avail		
Data	SHR_NDX	/u10/oracle/data/PROD/shr_ndx01.dbf	136	Avail		
Data	SYSTEM	/u03/oracle/data/PROD/system01.dbf	157	Avail		
Data	TEMP	/u11/oracle/data/PROD/temp01.dbf	262	Avail		
Data	TEMP_GL	/u15/oracle/data/PROD/temp_gl.dbf	210	Avail		
Data	TOOLS	/u03/oracle/data/PROD/tools01.dbf	16	Avail		
Data	USERS	/u20/oracle/data/PROD/users01.dbf	26	Avail		
Parm	Archive	/u05/oracle/admin/PROD/arch - ENABLED				
Parm	Ctrl 1	/u11/oracle/data/PROD/control01.ctl				
Parm	Ctrl 2	/u19/oracle/data/PROD/control02.ctl				
Parm	Ctrl 3	/u22/oracle/data/PROD/control03.ctl				
Parm	Ctrl 4	(none)				
Parm	Ifile	/u20/oracle/admin/PROD/pfile/configPROD.ora				
Redo	Grp 1	/u10/oracle/data/PROD/redo01.log	2	Curr	10243	no
Redo		/u21/oracle/data/PROD/redo01.log	2	Curr	10243	no
Redo	Grp 2	/u10/oracle/data/PROD/redo02.log	2	Inact	10241	YES
Redo		/u21/oracle/data/PROD/redo02.log	2	Inact	10241	YES
Redo	Grp 3	/u10/oracle/data/PROD/redo03.log	2	Inact	10242	YES
Red		/u21/oracle/data/PROD/redo03.log	2	Inact	10242	YES

```
      ************                                  ------
sum                                          6644
```

file_use.sql

Directory: *$DBA*
File Type: SQL Script
Edit Required: No
Output File: No

This script is called by the *file_use* script to create the report, as described in the previous section.

fixowner.sql

Directory: *$DBA*
File Type: SQL Script
Edit Required: No
Output File: *fix_own.sql*

This script creates a SQL script to fix the ownership of all primary keys that have a different owner from the table name that they are referencing, and a primary key that is referenced in a foreign key constraint. This situation has been known to cause ORA-00600 errors with an argument of 12838 to appear in trace dump files in some Oracle versions.

fixtable.sql

Directory: *$DBA*
File Type: SQL Script
Edit Required: No
Output File: *fixed.lis*

This script creates a SQL script (*cr_fixed.sql*) that contains a SELECT* from all of the X$ tables. This script is then executed to produce a report listing all values from the fixed tables, which can be used to locate which X$ table contains a specific value.

free

Directory: *$DBA*
File Type: Shell Script
Edit Required: No
Output File: *free.lis*
Syntax: free *[dbname]*

dbname

> Optional name of a database to be reported; if omitted, free space will be reported for all databases.

This shell script executes the *free.sql* script to create a report of all free space by tablespace for the specified database (or all databases). For each tablespace, the script prints the total bytes, bytes used, free bytes, and percent.

Sample report

```
                         FREE - Free space by Tablespace

                                                                    %
Tablespace Name       Total Bytes           Used             Free   Used
----------------     ------------------    ---------------   ---------------  ------
BRBS                    442,636,288         52,494,336       390,141,952   11.9
DBCARE                    5,242,880          2,398,208         2,844,672   45.7
DES2                     31,457,280         29,681,664         1,775,616   94.4
DES2_I                   20,971,520         20,832,256           139,264   99.3
RBS                     174,190,592         10,244,096       163,946,496    5.9
SYSTEM                  206,647,296        182,380,544        24,266,752   88.3
TEMPORARY_DATA          226,449,408              2,048       226,447,360    .0
TOOLS                    15,728,640          2,285,568        13,443,072   14.5
USERS                   508,674,048        499,437,568         9,236,480   98.2
USER_DATA             1,652,946,944      1,608,597,504        44,349,440   97.3
                     ------------------    ---------------   ---------------
sum                   3,284,944,896      2,408,353,792       876,591,104

10 rows selected.
```

free.sql

Directory: *$DBA*
File Type: SQL Script
Edit Required: No
Output File: *free.lst*

This script is called by the *free* script to create the report of free space in the database, as described in the previous section.

indcols

Directory: *$DBA*
File Type: Shell Script
Edit Required: No
Output File: *indcols.lis*

This shell script executes the *indcols.sql* script to create a report of all indexes (and the columns that comprise each index) for a given table. The script prompts the user for the database SID and the name of the table to be reported.

Sample report

```
INDCOLS - Indexes (and their columns) on table PRODUCT


Table Name                    Index Name                    Column Name
---------------------------   ---------------------------   --------------------
DDW.PRODUCT                   DDW.IND_PRODUCT_01            PROD_SEQ
                              DDW.IND_PRODUCT_02            PROD_NAME
LLARSON.PRODUCT              LLARSON.PRODUCT_INDEX        PRODID
```

instance.sql

Directory: *$DBA*
File Type: SQL Script
Edit Required: No
Output File: No

This script displays the date and time that the current instance was started. It must be executed by the SYS username on older versions of Oracle (since the V$INSTANCE view is only accessible by SYS.)

invalid

Directory: *$DBA*
File Type: Shell Script
Edit Required: No
Output File: Screen
Syntax: `invalid [sid]`

sid

    The Oracle SID of the database to be reported.

This script creates a report of all objects whose STATUS is not VALID. It also creates and then executes a script to try to recompile the invalid objects. It calls the *invalid.sql* script to create the report, as well as the script to perform the recompiling. Note that objects other than views are compiled by calling the DBMS_UTILITY.COMPILE_SCHEMA built-in procedure.

invalid.sql

Directory: *$DBA*
File Type: SQL Script
Edit Required: No
Output File: *invalid.is*

This script is called by the *invalid* script to create the report of invalid database objects, as described in the previous section.

istable.sql

Directory: *$DBA*
File Type: SQL Script
Edit Required: No
Output File: No
Syntax: `istable owner tablename`

owner
    The name of the schema that owns this table.

tablename
    The name of the table to be checked.

This script is used by various other scripts to verify that a specified table name is valid. It returns a status indicating whether or not a valid table was specified.

location

Directory: *$DBA*
File Type: Shell Script
Edit Required: No
Output File: Screen

This script creates a report displaying the location of all database files, parameter include files, and archive log files, grouped by directory, for all Oracle SIDs on the computer. File sizes are accumulated and totaled by directory. This script provides a convenient way to get a quick overview of all of the Oracle databases that are present on a system. It reads the *oratab* file to locate all of the Oracle SIDs. To gather that information, it requires that an existing OPS$username account be present in each database.

Sample report

```
10/27/97          Oracle database file locations, by directory          Page   1


                                                           MB
                                 Oracle                     on
Path / File Name                 SID      Type Tablespace  Disk   Stat
-------------------------------- -------- ---- ----------- ------ -----
                                 gb107p16 Parm Ifile          0 Good
app
  oracle
    admin
      dev
        pfile
                   configdev.ora  dev      Parm Ifile          0 Good
    product
      733
        dbs
                   arch           dev      Parm Archive          Disab
                   arch           gb107p16 Parm Archive          Disab
=======================> Subtotal for app ======== ==== Subtotal:          =====
oradata
  oradata
    dev
                   brbs01.dbf     dev      Data BRBS         322 Avail
                   brbs02.dbf     dev      Data BRBS         100 Avail
                   dbc01.dbf      dev      Data DBCARE         5 Avail
                   des2_data2     dev      Data DES2          10 Avail
                   des2data.dbf   dev      Data DES2          20 Avail
                   des2idx2.dbf   dev      Data DES2_I        10 Avail
                   des2indx.dbf   dev      Data DES2_I        10 Avail
                   rbs01.dbf      dev      Data RBS          116 Avail
                   rbs02.dbf      dev      Data RBS           50 Avail
                   sys2           dev      Data SYSTEM        50 Avail
                   system01.dbf   dev      Data SYSTEM        72 Avail
                   system03.dbf   dev      Data SYSTEM        75 Avail
                   tempdata.dbf   dev      Data TEMPORARY_DA 215 Avail
                                               TA

                   tools01.dbf    dev      Data TOOLS         15 Avail
                   userdata.dbf   dev      Data USER_DATA    740 Avail
                   userdata02.dbf dev      Data USER_DATA    736 Avail
                   userdata03.dbf dev      Data USER_DATA    100 Avail
                   users01.dbf    dev      Data USERS        485 Avail
                   control01.ctl  dev      Parm Ctrl 1         0 Good
                   control02.ctl  dev      Parm Ctrl 2         0 Good
                   control03.ctl  dev      Parm Ctrl 3         0 Good
                   redodev01.log  dev      Redo Grp 1         0 Inact
                   redodev02.log  dev      Redo Grp 2         0 Curr
                   redodev03.log  dev      Redo Grp 3         0 Inact
    gb107p16
                   data1.dbf      gb107p16 Data USER_DATA    300 Avail
                   data2.dbf      gb107p16 Data USER_DATA    200 Avail
                   data3.dbf      gb107p16 Data USER_DATA    100 Avail
                   data4.dbf      gb107p16 Data USER_DATA    100 Avail
                   data5.dbf      gb107p16 Data USER_DATA     75 Avail
```

```
                       index1.dbf          gb107p16 Data USER_INDEX      200 Avail
                       index2.dbf          gb107p16 Data USER_INDEX      100 Avail
                       index3.dbf          gb107p16 Data USER_INDEX      100 Avail
                       index4.dbf          gb107p16 Data USER_INDEX       50 Avail
                       index5.dbf          gb107p16 Data USER_INDEX       75 Avail
                       office.dbf          gb107p16 Data OFFICE           50 Avail
                       rbs.dbf             gb107p16 Data RBS             100 Avail
                       system1.dbf         gb107p16 Data SYSTEM          300 Avail
                       system2.dbf         gb107p16 Data SYSTEM          200 Avail
                       system3.dbf         gb107p16 Data SYSTEM           75 Avail
                       system4.dbf         gb107p16 Data SYSTEM          100 Avail
                       temp.dbf            gb107p16 Data TEMP            100 Avail
                       cntrlgb107p16.dbf   gb107p16 Parm Ctrl 1            0 Good
                       log1.dbf            gb107p16 Redo Grp 3            10 Unuse
                       log2.dbf            gb107p16 Redo Grp 2            10 Unuse
                       log3.dbf            gb107p16 Redo Grp 1            10 Curr
==================> Subtotal for oradata ======== ==== Subtotal:        5386 =====

******************************************* ******** **** Grand Total:   5386 *****
```

locate2.sql

Directory: *$DBA*
File Type: SQL Script
Edit Required: No
Output File: *location.lis*

This script is called by the *location* script to create the report of database file locations. See the *location* script for details.

mport

Directory: *$DBA*
File Type: Shell Script
Edit Required: Optional
Output File: *mport.log*
Syntax: mport *sid dest_file*

sid
    The Oracle SID for the database into which this script will import.

dest_file
    The filespec for the export file to be imported.

This script implements a generic full database import procedure, used when importing one database's export data into a different database. As written, it imports the data file specified by the second argument *(dest_file)* into the dbname database. The script does the following:

1. Shuts down the database.

2. Opens it in exclusive mode.

3. Imports the data.

4. Shuts down the database.

All import activity is logged in the file *mport.log*.

For example, to import an EXPort file from the PRD1 database (which is named */usr/backup/PRD1.dmp)* into the TEST database, specify the following:

```
mport
test /usr/backup/PRD1.dmp
```

Note that you can edit this script to permit a backup filesystem structure that is implemented at your site.

nondata.sql

Directory: *$DBA*
File Type: SQL Script
Edit Required: No
Output File: Screen

This script lists all of the nondata objects within a database. Nondata objects are all objects other than tables, indexes, clusters, and rollback segments.

products

Directory: *$DBA*
File Type: Shell Script
Edit Required: No
Output File: Screen

This shell script lists all of the installed Oracle products, versions, filenames, and dates of installation.

Sample report

```
              Report of all Installed Oracle Products on syst01

Version      Filename Product                              Installed
-----------  -------- -----------------------------------  --------------------
4.0.1.0.0    orainst  Oracle UNIX Installer                04/23/97 10:19:43 AM
1.0.1.0.0    oraview  Oracle On-Line Text Viewer           04/23/97 10:18:32 AM
7.3.3.0.0    nlsrtl_common ORACLE NLS Libraries and Utiliti 04/23/97 10:20:44 AM
7.3.3.0.0    oracore_common ORACLE Core Libraries          04/23/97 10:20:49 AM
7.3.3.0.0    rdbms_common ORACLE Common RDBMS Libraries and 04/23/97 10:22:14 AM
7.3.3.0.0    plsql_common ORACLE PL/SQL Libraries          04/23/97 10:21:35 AM
7.3.3.0.0    slax_common ORACLE Common Libraries           04/23/97 10:20:52 AM
7.3.3.0.0    precomp_common ORACLE Common Precomp Libraries 04/23/97 10:20:57 AM
7.3.3.0.0    network_common ORACLE Common Network Libraries 04/23/97 10:21:17 AM
```

```
7.3.3.0.0    otrace_common ORACLE Common Trace Libraries      04/23/97 10:21:03 AM
7.3.3.0.0    buildtools_common ORACLE Common Utilities        04/23/97 10:19:59 AM
7.3.3.0.0    ocommon   ORACLE Common Libraries and Utilities  04/23/97 10:22:16 AM
7.3.3.0.0    platform_common Platform specific Libraries an   04/23/97 10:19:49 AM
2.3.3.0.0    network   SQL*Net (V2)                           04/23/97 10:23:04 AM
2.3.3.0.0    tcppa     TCP/IP Protocol Adapter (V2)           04/23/97 10:23:09 AM
1.3.3.0.0    rpc       Remote Operations                      04/23/97 10:22:23 AM
2.0.3.0.0    names     Oracle Names                           04/23/97 10:26:06 AM
2.1.4.14.0   tk21      ToolKit 2.1 Base                       04/23/97 10:25:38 AM
2.3.6.4.0    tk23      ToolKit 2.3 Base                       05/09/97 11:51:09 AM
7.3.3.0.0    slax      SLAX: parser                           04/23/97 10:32:37 AM
2.3.3.0.0    plsql     PL/SQL V2                               04/23/97 10:26:28 AM
7.3.3.0.0    ddbo      ORACLE7 Distributed Database option    04/23/97 10:26:31 AM
7.3.3.0.0    pqo       ORACLE7 Parallel Query option          04/23/97 10:26:34 AM
2.3.3.0.0    svrmgr    Oracle Server Manager                  04/23/97 10:27:23 AM
7.3.3.0.0    rdbms     ORACLE7 Server (RDBMS)                 04/23/97 10:30:53 AM
7.3.3.0.0    md        Spatial Data Option                    04/23/97 10:31:56 AM
1.0.0.0.1    dbup      <Database Startup> Load Files          04/23/97 10:30:57 AM
7.3.3.0.0    xa        ORACLE7 XA Library                     04/23/97 10:32:34 AM
7.3.3        otrace    Oracle Trace                           04/23/97 10:30:52 AM
7.3.3.0.0    precomp   Precomp                                04/23/97 10:32:46 AM
2.2.3.0.0    proc      Pro*C                                  04/23/97 10:33:01 AM
2.1.0.0.0    ows21     Oracle WebServer                       04/23/97 02:34:03 PM
3.3.3.0.0    plus      SQL*Plus                               04/23/97 10:31:14 AM
2.1.4.14.0   tk21      ToolKit 2.1 Extension                  04/23/97 10:33:12 AM
2.3.6.4.0    tk23      ToolKit 2.3 Extension                  05/09/97 11:51:36 AM
2.0.5.4.0    mm2       Multimedia APIs                        04/23/97 10:33:16 AM
2.0.7.7.1    mm2       Multimedia APIs                        05/09/97 11:51:51 AM
2.0.0.11.1   ca20      Tools Common Area                      05/09/97 11:51:57 AM
1.5.6.15.0   de15      PL/SQL Procedure Builder               05/09/97 11:53:03 AM
1.2.0.3.0    nn12      Integration Services                   05/09/97 11:53:06 AM
2.1.1.0.0    hh2       Oracle Help                            04/23/97 10:33:24 AM
2.1.5.2.1    hh2       Oracle Help                            05/09/97 11:52:06 AM
2.1.10.6.1   vgs21     Virtual Graphics System                05/09/97 11:53:33 AM
2.2.2.0.4    book22    Oracle Book                            05/09/97 11:55:42 AM
2.5.6.2.2    ocl25     Oracle Charting Library                05/09/97 11:56:00 AM
2.5.7.0.0    og25      Oracle Graphics                        05/09/97 11:57:37 AM
4.5.7.1.2    forms45   Oracle Forms                           05/09/97 12:01:08 PM
2.5.5.4.0    or25      Oracle Reports                         05/09/97 12:05:58 PM
2.1.3.0.0    oacore2   Oracle Office Automation Core          04/23/97 10:33:36 AM
2.0.9.3.1    browser20 Oracle Browser                         05/09/97 12:08:21 PM
2.3.3.0.0    svrmgr    Oracle Server Manager (Motif)          04/23/97 10:34:15 AM
```

renamcol.sql

Directory: *$DBA*
File Type: SQL Script
Edit Required: No
Output File: No

This script renames an existing column in a table. This does not require the table to be recreated.

WARNING	Use this script with extreme caution. Renaming columns is not supported by current versions of Oracle, and this script accomplishes the task by modifying the data dictionary. DBA privilege is required. You must shut down the database and restart it immediately after executing this script in order to flush the System Global Area (SGA).

resize

Directory: *$DBA*
File Type: Shell Script
Edit Required: No
Output File: *re_size.sql*

This script generates a script containing DDL statements that can be used to resize an existing table so that all existing data. will fit into a single extent. This script assumes that no foreign key constraints exist for the table.

WARNING	You must manually delete any existing copy of *re_size.sql* before running this script. If *re_size.sql* exists, an error message will be generated and the script will end.

tabanal

Directory: *$DBA*
File Type: Shell Script
Edit Required: No
Output File: *tabanal.lis*

This script prints a detailed analysis of a specific tablespace. It is used when the free space in a tablespace is getting too low, and you want to see what types of records are filling up the tablespace.

The report first lists all of the tables and indexes in the specified tablespace. The objects are ordered in descending order of bytes allocated. For each of the tables, the average row size and the number of rows are calculated and printed. If there is a column of a DATE datatype within each table, the number of rows are calculated and grouped by the first DATE field that is found. This can help determine the frequency of new growth for each of the listed tables.

This script executes the following scripts to gather the information and create the report: *tabanal.sql, tabanaln.sql, tabanali.sql, tabanalt, tabanali, tabanala.sql, tabanald.sql, tabanalc.sql, tabanalv.sql,* and *tabanale.sql.* Since these scripts are internal support routines, they are not documented here but are commented in the script source files.

NOTE   An OPS$username account must exist in the specified database and it needs SELECT access to the dba_segments and dba_tab_columns data dictionary views.

Sample report

```
Analysis of GENERAL_TABLES tablespace for PROD1 database

Owner          Name                          Type          Bytes    Extents
-----------    ---------------------------   --------   -----------  ---------
APPSCH1        MASTER_DETAIL                 TABLE       21,135,360        17
APPSCH1        CUSTOMER_GROUP                TABLE        5,242,880         3
APPSCH1        CUSTOMER_TYPE                 TABLE        1,105,920         1
                                                        ------------
sum                                                      27,484,160

           Distribution by CREATE_DATE date for APPSCH1.MASTER_DETAIL table
           (Average row size is 264 bytes)

                           CREATE_DATE        Count     K-Bytes
-----------------------    ---------------------   ---------   ------------
                              97/06/23        1976         509
                              97/06/24        2013         519
                              97/06/25        2080         536
                              97/06/26        1997         515
                              97/06/27        2087         538
                              97/06/28        2003         516
                              97/06/29        1983         511
                                             -------    ----------
sum                                          40651      10,480

Distribution for APPSCH1.CUSTOMER_GROUP table
           (Average row size is 13 bytes)

                                 Date        Count     K-Bytes
-----------------------    ---------------------   ---------   ------------
                                (n/a)          10           0
                                             -------    ----------
sum                                            10           0

Distribution for APPSCH1.CUSTOMER_TYPE table
           (Average row size is 12 bytes)
```

	Date	Count	K-Bytes
----------------------- -----------------------	---------	-------------	
	(n/a)	3	0
		-------	----------
sum		3	0

tableown

Directory: *$DBA*
File Type: Shell Script
Edit Required: No
Output File: Screen

This script provides a very quick method of reporting the owner and tablespace name for a given table. The user is prompted for the Oracle SID and table name.

tableown.sql

Directory: *$DBA*
File Type: SQL Script
Edit Required: No
Output File: Screen

This script is called by the *tableown* script to display the list of table owners and tablespaces.

tablesp.sql

Directory: *$DBA*
File Type: SQL Script
Edit Required: No
Output File: *tablesp.lis*

This script creates a report of the allocated, used, and free space for every tablespace. Note that a temporary table, t*ablesp_tmp*, is created for use in collecting statistics for this script.

tablstat

Directory: *$DBA*
File Type: Shell Script
Edit Required: No
Output File: *tablstat.lis*
Syntax: tablstat *tablename*

tablename

The name of the table to be reported.

This script is used by the DBA to view all of the relevant statistics pertaining to an individual table. It prints a report containing the following statistics:

- Number of rows
- Number of bytes
- DB_BLOCK_SIZE
- PCTFREE
- Percent of distinct columns (optional)
- Indexed columns for a specified table
- Constraints about a specified table

This information is useful for determining whether an index should or should not be created on one or more columns of a table. This script executes the *tablstat.sql* and *tablecon.sql* scripts to gather the data and print the report.

Restrictions

- The ORACLE_SID environment variable must be set.
- An OPS$username account must exist in the database.
- In order to calculate the percentage of the distinct columns, the Oracle built-in package DBMS_SQL, must exist and be executable by this username. Note that for large tables, the calculation of distinct column percentages may take a while to run, since the script will make one pass through the database for each of the table's columns.

Sample report

```
prod table PROD1.PCMCORE contains 2071 rows in
   466,944 bytes, DB_BLOCK_SIZE of  2048 PCTFREE of     10
```

			Percent distinct
Column	Datatype	Length	values
---	---	---	---
WAFER_NAME	VARCHAR2	17	65%
LOT_ID	VARCHAR2	10	24%
PROCESS_TYPE	VARCHAR2	50	1%
PROC_STAGE	VARCHAR2	15	0%
MEAS_NO	NUMBER	(3)	0%
MEASUR_DATE	DATE	7	18%
MASK_NAME	VARCHAR2	20	6%
OPERATOR	VARCHAR2	30	1%

COMMENT1	VARCHAR2	80	5%
COMMENT2	VARCHAR2	80	1%
RGO100F	NUMBER	(8,1)	21%
RGO200F	NUMBER	(8,1)	33%
RCONT	NUMBER	(7,2)	5%
RSECONT	NUMBER	(7,2)	72%
FIT	NUMBER	(8,1)	91%
RTR50	NUMBER	(7,2)	35%
RTR25	NUMBER	(7,2)	23%
CAPZERO	NUMBER	(6,2)	28%
ABGOOD	NUMBER	(3)	0%
ABSHORT	NUMBER	(3)	0%
ABOC	NUMBER	(3)	0%

```
        Unique Index PCMCORE_1 on WAFER_NAME
                             LOT_ID
                             PROC_STAGE
                             MEAS_NO
```

Besides showing the table's structure and its count of distinct columns, this report indicates that there is a single unique index on three concatenated columns.

```
prod table PROD1.PROGRAM contains 124 rows in
    10,240 bytes, DB_BLOCK_SIZE of  2048 PCTFREE of    10
```

			Percent
distinct			
Column	Datatype	Length	values
----------------------------	------------------	---------	---------
TASK	VARCHAR2	35	100%
PROGRAM	VARCHAR2	12	21%
MANAGER	VARCHAR2	9	0%
WIPACCT#	VARCHAR2	10	23%
CHARGE_NO	VARCHAR2	10	90%
STATUS	VARCHAR2	8	2%
STATUS_DATE	DATE	7	12%
VALIDWHO	VARCHAR2	10	3%

```
        Unique Index PROG_PK on TASK
        Foreign key on MANAGER
            references PROD1.OPERATOR
                        USER_ID
        Not Null on TASK
```

In addition to showing the table's structure and its count of distinct columns, the preceding report indicates that there is a single unique index on the first column, a foreign key on manager (which references the USER_ID in the PROD1.OPERATOR table), and a NOT NULL constraint on the TASK column.

tablstat.sql

Directory: *$DBA*
File Type: SQL Script
Edit Required: Optional
Output File: *tablstat.lis*

This script is called by the *tablstat* script to create the report of table statistics displayed. See the *tablstat* script for sample output.

tblsize.sql

Directory: *$DBA*
File Type: SQL Script
Edit Required: Optional
Output File: See Below

This script is used when you are creating a new database. After specifying the minimal amount of data (via SQL INSERT statements) included in the beginning of this file, the script executes the *tblsize.sql* script.

The *tblsize.sql* script creates three different output files:

tblsize.lst
> A report describing the complete configuration and sizing information regarding all of the tables, indexes, and tablespaces.

tblspddl.sql
> A SQL script containing DDL that, when executed, can be used to create all of the correctly sized tablespaces.

tblddl.sql
> A SQL script containing DDL that, when executed, can be used to create all of the correctly sized tables and indexes. It can optionally execute a separate script to create any desired constraints or triggers on the tables.

Detailed comments, as well as sample data, are included in the distributed *tblsize.sql* script. Some database-wide definitions are specified in "def" statements. You must remove or change the INSERT statements to describe the database that you are creating. The script requires access to the Oracle built-in package, DBMS_OUTPUT.

Parameters

The data is specified in the *tblsize.sql* script in the following variables:

blksize
> Defines the DB_BLOCK_SIZE of the database that is to be created.

INITRANS

> Values for the table and the index are specified in the initrans_table and initrans_index variables.

ddl_table

> Set to 1 if you want to include the DDL definitions for the tables in the output files.

ddl_index

> Set to 1 if you want to include the DDL definitions for the indexes in the output files.

ddl_synonym

> Set to 1 if you want to include the DDL definitions to automatically create public synonyms for all of the tables in the output files.

ddl_tablespace

> Set to 1 if you want to include the DDL definitions for the tablespaces in the output files.

ddl_raw variable

> Set to 1 if the database's data files will be placed on raw devices, or 0 if they will be placed on filesystems.

limit_extents

> Can be used to constrain the size of each table or index so that there will be a reasonable chance that the table being created can actually fit into an existing tablespace.

If limit_extents is set to 1, the INITIAL and NEXT extent clauses will be constrained so that each extent is no more than 95% of the average contiguous bytes in the tablespace (so that there is a reasonable chance that the table can actually be created in an existing tablespace), and so that each extent is no more than 50% of the smallest number of bytes in each data file comprising the tablespace (so the table can always grow to at least two extents within a single data file).

If limit_extents is set to 0, the INITIAL and NEXT extent clauses will be calculated so they contain all of the specified data in a single extent, regardless of whether or not any existing tablespace has enough free space within it to support that size.

Tables

The next section of the script describes each of the tables to be created in the database. For each table, eight values are specified in each INSERT statement:

*   The owner name (schema) of the table

*   The name of the table

- The tablespace name to contain the table

- The tablespace name to contain the table's indexes; if no tablespace name is specified, the table's tablespace name will be used with a suffix of *_IDX* appended to it

- The PCTFREE value for the table

- The PCTUSED value for the table

- The maximum number of rows to size the INITIAL extent of the table; unless constrained by the limit_extents parameter or by the size of a UNIX filesystem, the table will be sized to store all of the specified rows in the initial extent of the table

- The number of additional rows to be inserted into this table each month

Average row size

The next section is optional. If it is included, it specifies the average size of each row for the specified tables, overriding the program's usual calculations of the average row size based upon the "Average number of digits or characters for each column" values in the following section's definitions. This is used when it would be too much trouble to specify the average number of digits or characters in every column of every table, so that the program can correctly calculate the size of an average row in each table. For each table, two values are specified in each INSERT statement:

- The name of the table

- The average row size (in bytes) for the table

Columns

The next section describes each of the columns in each of the tables. For each column, the following values are specified in each INSERT statement:

- The name of the table

- The name of the column in the table

- The datatype of the column. It must be one of the following five values:

  — nx = NUMBER datatype (where x is the number of digits)

  — vx = VARCHAR2 datatype (where x is the maximum number of characters)

  — cx = CHAR datatype (where x is the number of characters)

  — d = DATE datatype

  — l = LONG datatype

- The average number of characters if the column is a VARCHAR2 or LONG datatype, or the average number of digits if the column is a NUMBER datatype. This column's value is ignored if the column is any other datatype.

- The number of decimal digits if the column is a NUMBER datatype. This column's value is ignored if the column is not a NUMBER datatype.

Column constraints

The next section describes the column constraints on any column of any table. This section is optional; if there are no column constraints, there will be no entries for this section. Due to the amount of text required for constraints, typically only NOT NULL constraints are specified in this section. Use the optional *constraints.sql* script to specify all other constraints (such as referential integrity constraints). For each constraint, three values are specified in each INSERT statement:

- The name of the table

- The name of the column in the table

- The actual text of the constraint

DEFAULT value clauses

The next section describes the DEFAULT value clause to be placed on any column of any table. This section is optional; if there are no DEFAULT clauses, there will be no entries for this section. For each DEFAULT clause, three values are specified in each INSERT statement:

- The name of the table

- The name of the column in the table

- The actual value to be specified as the DEFAULT value for the column

Indexes

The last section describes all of the indexes to be placed on each table. This section is optional, although most databases will require indexes for good performance. For each index, six values are specified in each INSERT statement:

- The name of the table

- The name of the index; if no index name is specified, the table's name will be used, with a prefix of IND_ and a suffix consisting of the index sequence number (as described in the fifth column of the INSERT statement)

- The name of the column to be included in the index

- The sequence number of the index; the sequence number is a sequential number used to separate different indexes; the first index on a table should have a sequence number of 1, the second one should have a sequence number of 2, and so on

- The type of the index; it must be one of the following values:
  - p = primary key index
  - u = unique index
  - b = bitmap index
  - I = nonunique index

- The position number of the column in a concatenated index; for indexes consisting of multiple columns in a single index, the first column should have a value of 1, the second column should have a value of 2, and so on; for indexes consisting of just a single column, specify 1 for this field

tblsizec.sql

Directory: *$DBA*
File Type: SQL Script
Edit Required: No
Output File: *inserts.sql*

This script creates another script (*inserts.sql*) that contains the INSERT statements required by the *tblsize.sql* script described in the previous section (except for the initial number of rows and growth per month for each table, and any constraints other than NOT NULL).

You can run this script for an existing small "test" database, which has the identical structure as a large "production" database that you are planning to create. Doing this will save lots of the typing necessary to properly run the *tblsize.sql* script when creating a differently-sized database from the existing one. This script prompts you for the schema whose data dictionary information is to be accessed. It requires read access to the DBA_TABLES, DBA_TAB_COLUMNS, DBA_INDEXES, and DBA_IND_COLUMNS data dictionary tables. It also requires that the DBMS_OUTPUT package exist and be executable. To use the use_current_size parameter, Oracle 7.2.2.3 or later is required, since the DBMS_SQL package must exist and be executable by the current username.

Be sure to set the use_current_size parameter before running this script. Settings have the following meanings:

- If use_current_size is set to 1, this script will count the number of rows in each table, calculate the average row size of each table, use the current number of rows as the initial number of rows, and use the average row size value when calculating table sizes.

- If use_current_size is set to 0, this script will use the default_initial parameter as the initial number of rows and use the maximum size of each column as its average size.

See the *tblsize.sql* script documentation for more details.

xport

Directory: *$DBA*
File Type: Shell Script
Edit Required: Optional
Output File: No
Syntax: xport *sid dest_file*

sid
> The Oracle SID of the database to be exported.

dest_file
> The full name of the export file.

This script is a generic full database export procedure, used when exporting a database. As written, it exports the dbname database to an export file named in the second argument (dest_file). This script can be used with the corresponding import script to import the exported data into another database.

9

Database Developer Utilities

The scripts in this section allow application developers and DBAs to create EXPLAIN PLAN reports of SQL statements quite easily. EXPLAIN PLAN is an Oracle tool that allows you to view the access path that Oracle will use when a specific SQL statement is executed, without having to actually execute the statement. This allows developers and DBAs to optimize the SQL statement for the best performance.

This chapter also includes scripts for use with the Revision Control System (RCS), a UNIX utility which allows developers to "check in" code to an RCS library. The code can then be "checked out" in order to make changes. When the code is subsequently checked back in again, a new version of the code is created. At any time, the current or previous version of the code can be retrieved for examination or subsequent modifications.

The scripts described in this chapter comprise a suite of tools that provide developers with an easy-to-use interface to the RCS utilities provided on most UNIX platforms. For full documentation, see the *rcs.doc* file.

This chapter also describes a set of easy-to-use front-end scripts for using RCS to manage source code. RCS provides a standard set of UNIX commands to allow source code to be managed by a central source code library. By controlling access and updates to the application source code, security is enhanced and errors are reduced. Since each update to the source code creates a new version within RCS, errors that have been introduced by an update to the code can be easily reversed by retrieving and installing a prior version.

autoplan.sql

Directory: *$TOOLS*
File Type: SQL Script
Edit Required: Optional
Output File: *autoplan.lis*

This script can be used by developers and DBAs to automatically generate EXPLAIN PLAN output for the current SQL statement. With the SQL statement that you want to analyze in the buffer (either by typing in the desired SQL statement or by using the SQL*Plus GET command), you can invoke autoplan as follows:

```
@autoplan
```

An EXPLAIN PLAN of the SQL statement will be performed and then displayed. After the report is displayed, the original SQL statement will be left intact in the SQL buffer.

Restrictions

- The user needs DBA privileges or SELECT access to V_$SESSION. To grant this privilege as user SYS, type the following:

  ```
  GRANT SELECT ON V_$SESSION TO PUBLIC.
  ```

- The *autoplan.sql* script must reside in the current directory, or anywhere in the ORACLE_PATH environment variable. This will allow easy execution by simply typing the following at any SQL*Plus prompt:

  ```
  @autoplan
  ```

- The PLAN_TABLE must already exist in the user's schema. To create the PLAN_TABLE, run the following SQL*Plus command from the user's account:

  ```
  @$ORACLE_HOME/rdbms/admin/utlxplan
  ```

The COST, BYTES, and CARDINALITY columns are available only in Oracle 7.3 and above; if you are using this script with an earlier Oracle version, you will have to modify the script to remove these columns from the report.

Sample report

This is a report for the following SQL statement:

```
select product_code from pob.product where org_code < 123;
```

Obj Level	Operation	Object	Ins	Opt Plan	Cost	# rows	# Byte
1.0	SELECT STATEMENT			Choo			
2.1	TBL ACCESS FULL	POB.PRODUCT	1				

TIP   Plan tables are often difficult for even experienced DBAs and devel-
              opers to understand, and the contents are not well-documented by
              Oracle. For the most complete treatment of the subject, see Chapter
              10 in *Advanced Oracle Tuning and Administration* by Eyal Aronoff,
              Kevin Loney, and Noorali Sonawalla (Oracle Press, 1997).

history

Directory: *$DBA*

File Type: Shell Script

Edit Required: No

Output File: Screen

Syntax: `history [program_name]`

program_name
> The name of the program whose history is to be displayed; if omitted, the his-
> tory of all programs in the RCS library will be displayed.

This script displays the history of one or more programs from an RCS source directory tree.

Restrictions

- The environment variable RCSLIBR must have been previously defined by
  means of the *lib* command.

- To create or access an RCS library, the user must be in the "rcssys" group,
  and the library's parent directory must have read/write access for the "rcssys"
  group.

lib

Directory: *$TOOLS*

File Type: Shell Script

Edit Required: No

Output File: No

The *lib* script defines the RCS library environment variable, so that the other RCS
scripts can access the correct RCS library. For full documentation, see the *rcs.doc*
file.

To execute this script, first set the environment variable L to the PATH of the directory that contains the RCS library to be accessed. Then, type the following to define the required RCS environment variable:

```
.lib
```

rcs.doc

Directory: *$TOOLS*
File Type: Shell Script
Edit Required: No
Output File: No

This file contains the full documentation for all of the RCS scripts (*history, lib, replace, reserve, reservs,* and *unreserv*).

replace

Directory: *$TOOLS*
File Type: Shell Script
Edit Required: No
Output File: No
Syntax: `replace` *program_name*

program_name
    The name of the program to be inserted or replaced.

This script inserts or replaces a program in an RCS library. The name of the program is specified in the argument. Full documentation is contained in the *rcs.doc* file.

Restrictions

- The environment variable RCSLIBR must have been previously defined by means of the *lib* command.

- To create or access an RCS library, the user must be in the "rcssys" group, and the library's parent directory must have read/write access for the "rcssys" group.

reserve

Directory: *$TOOLS*
File Type: Shell Script
Edit Required: No
Output File: No
Syntax: `reserve [-r] [-f] [-s xxx] program_name`

-r

> This argument will "RCS lock" the code. This is required if you are retrieving the program to make modifications to it. The "lock" will prevent other users from modifying the code at the same time you are modifying it. If the *-r* argument is not specified, the program is checked out without locking it (allowing anyone else to check out the same program at the same time).

-f

> This argument indicates that the code should not be locked.

-s xxx

> This argument is used to specify a particular revision (version) of the source code to be retrieved. If this argument is not specified, the latest version of the source code will be retrieved.

program_name

> The program to be checked out.

This script is used to "check out" a program from an RCS library. If neither the *-r* nor the *-f* argument is specified, the script will prompt you regarding whether or not you want to lock the program.

Restrictions

- The environment variable RCSLIBR must have been previously defined by means of the *lib* command.

- To create or access an RCS library, the user must be in the "rcssys" group, and the library's parent directory must have read/write access for the "rcssys" group.

- The mode script must exist and be found in the PATH.

reservs

Directory: *$TOOLS*
File Type: Shell Script
Edit Required: No
Output File: No

This script displays a report of all programs that are "RCS locked" in the current RCS library. For full documentation, see the *rcs.doc* file.

Restrictions

- The environment variable RCSLIBR must have been previously defined by using the *lib* command.

- To create or access an RCS library, the user must be in the "rcssys" group, and the library's parent directory must have read/write access for the "rcssys" group.

unreserv

Directory: *$TOOLS*
File Type: Shell Script
Edit Required: No
Output File: No

This script "unlocks" code that was previously locked in an RCS library. Use this script if you change your mind about modifying a program that you previously "RCS locked" with the reserve script. For full documentation, see the *rcs.doc* file.

Restrictions

- The environment variable RCSLIBR must have been previously defined by using the *lib* command.

- To create or access an RCS library, the user must be in the "rcssys" group, and the library's parent directory must have read/write access for the "rcssys" group.

- The *mode* script must exist and be found in the PATH.

IV

UNIX Utility Scripts

This part of the book contains a collection of scripts that perform UNIX-level functions that both Oracle DBAs and developers will find helpful. Many of these scripts are also called by other scripts in this book.

10

General System Utilities

This chapter contains a set of UNIX utilities that perform a variety of general-purpose functions. Many of the other scripts described in this book execute these scripts to perform the following functions:

- Perform an auto-logoff program for inactive Oracle database users
- Calculate *n* days offset from the current date
- Return the operating system type (to support vendor-specific code)
- Kill the UNIX processes that contain a specific string in the username or command field
- Print an 80- or 132-column portrait-mode report to an HP LaserJet printer
- Return the UNIX mode protection value for a file
- Display a list of all files that have been modified in the last 24 hours
- Display the amount of physical memory
- Replace the old definition of an environment variable within the PATH with a new definition
- Remove trailing white space (blanks or tabs) from a file

dbakill

Directory: *$DBA*
File Type: Shell Script
Edit Required: No
Output File: Screen

This script is the executable version of the *dbakill.c* script described in the next section. It is executed by the *killunix* script to kill specific sessions that are accessing the Oracle database.

dbakill.c

Directory: *$DBA*
File Type: Source Code
Edit Required: No
Output File: Screen

This file contains the source program for the *dbakill* script described in the previous section. It is used to execute the UNIX *kill-9* command with root privileges. This command can be used to allow the "oracle" user to kill all sessions that might be accessing an Oracle database, even if the username is not "oracle."

getsyi

Directory: *$TOOLS*
File Type: Shell Script
Edit Required: No
Output File: Screen

This script returns the name of the current operating system. Since each vendor's UNIX commands may operate somewhat differently, scripts containing those commands need to know on which operating system they are executing. This is done by calling this script and taking appropriate action based upon the value returned.

Note that this script executes the system's *hostname* and *uname* commands in order to obtain the required information. Therefore, these commands must be found in the PATH. Interactive sessions usually have these commands included in the PATH. For noninteractive (i.e., *cron*) jobs, the *dbabatch* file ensures that the required directory (typically, */etc*) is in the PATH. If your system's *hostname* and *uname* commands are located in a different directory, you should change the *dbabatch* file to include the required directory in the PATH.

killunix

Directory: *$DBA*
File Type: Shell Script
Edit Required: No
Output File: Screen

This script kills the UNIX process(es) that contain the specified string ($1) in the *ps -ef* display's command field or username. It does not kill the process that is executing this script. This script is executed by the *backup* script to terminate any left-over sessions that might exist. It uses any third-party */etc/pbrun* utility or *$DBA/ dbakill* program to execute the *kill* command, if it exists.

mailto

Directory: *$TOOLS*
File Type: Shell Script
Edit Required: No
Output File: Screen

This script is a template that can be used to mail the contents of the specified parameter (text or file) to specific users (such as the DBA or UNIX system administration staff). Electronic mail is a very useful method for notifying DBA(s) and other personnel of current or pending database problems. If a common interface script is used for all such communication, site-specific modifications (such as sending all mail to a pager) can be easily incorporated and facilitated without having to change the many applications and scripts that send mail.

You will need to edit this script so it conforms to your site's user names and mail system interface. As mentioned, the script can be modified to interface with a dial-up pager or other notification system (assuming that you have the appropriate software installed on the system).

replpath

Directory: *$TOOLS*
File Type: Shell Script
Edit Required: No
Output File: Screen

This script is used to replace the old definition of an environment variable within the PATH with a new definition. It is executed by the *$DBA/define* script.

trunc

Directory: *$TOOLS*
File Type: Shell Script
Edit Required: No
Output File: Screen

This script is used to remove any trailing white space (blanks or tab characters) from the specified file. It is particularly useful for trimming the extra space in SQL*Plus fixed-length spool output files.

11

Directory and File Management Utilities

Even though Oracle DBAs are focused primarily on events within a database, there are many times when they will need to manipulate UNIX operating system files. This commonly occurs when databases are being backed up or restored.

The scripts described in this chapter can be used to copy and compress files, define required parameters for DBA-related scripts, define a temporary scratch file name, restore and uncompress files, and calculate when a file was created.

copy_log

Directory: *$DBA*
File Type: Shell Script
Edit Required: Yes
Output File: Screen

This script is called by the *$DBA/backup* script to perform the actual backing up of the database files.

WARNING   This script is site-specific and may need to be changed to integrate with your own site's backup method(s).

---

days_old

Directory: *$TOOLS*
File Type: Shell Script
Edit Required: No
Output File: Screen

This script calculates and returns the age (in days) of the specified file ($FILE) in a shell variable called DAYS_OLD. A value of -1 is returned if the specified file does not exist.

dbabatch

Directory: *$HOME*
File Type: Shell Script
Edit Required: Yes
Output File: Screen

This script defines the required parameters for the DBA-related scripts. You will need to move all of the non-terminal definitions into this file from the "oracle" user's *.profile* file. This allows *cron* "batch" jobs to call this script file without any errors (since *cron* jobs do not have a terminal associated with them.)

Most important, this script defines the DBA and TOOLS environment variables, which are used to locate all of the other scripts, and inserts these definitions into the PATH. You can also define additional variables, such as EDITOR, ORACLE_TERM, and TERM, in this file.

This file must be located in the "oracle" user's home directory. It is always called from that user's *.profile* file, as in the following:

```
./dbabatch
```

mktemp

Directory: *$TOOLS*
File Type: Shell Script
Edit Required: No
Output File: Screen

This script is provided as a substitute "mktemp" command for UNIX systems that do not have their own *mktemp* command. It is used to create a unique temporary scratch file name. It is called by many of the other scripts when a temporary filename needs to be created.

rest_log

Directory: *$DBA*
File Type: Shell Script
Edit Required: No
Output File: Screen
Syntax: `rest_log` *source_file dest_file*

source_file
> The name of the file to be copied.

dest_file
> The name of the file to which source_file is to be copied.

This script is used to copy/uncompresses a file. You must specify both a source and a destination file name. This script is used only if a *restore_<sid>* script is created by the *creback* script.

12

Memory Usage Reports

This chapter contains several scripts for UNIX systems. One displays all of the memory statistics for an HP-UX computer system. Another displays the amount of available free system memory for Sun or HP-UX systems. Typically, these scripts are used to debug memory usage for a given application or process. If you execute them before and after the desired process to be monitored, you will notice any change in the memory utilization.

These scripts are used by the backup scripts to allow errors pertaining to memory exhaustion to be spotted and diagnosed more easily.

allmemry

Directory: *$DBA*
File Type: Shell Script
Edit Required: No
Output File: Screen

This script displays all HP-UX memory statistics. It is called by the *backup* script to include debugging information in the daily backup log file. The script executes the *allmemry.exe* script to obtain the memory statistics, and it compiles the *allmemry.c* script into *allmemry.exe*, if *allmemry.exe* does not exist.

allmemry.c

Directory: *$DBA*
File Type: Source Code
Edit Required: No
Output File: Screen

This file contains HP-UX source code for the *allmemry.exe* script described in the previous section. It is compiled by the *allmemry* script if *allmemry.exe* does not exist.

freemem

Directory: *$DBA*
File Type: Shell Script
Edit Required: No
Output File: Screen

This script displays the amount of free memory (in megabytes or kilobytes) for Sun and HP-UX systems. See the comments within the script regarding customization options.

freemem.c

Directory: *$DBA*
File Type: Source Code
Edit Required: No
Output File: Screen

This file contains the source code for the free memory display for HP-UX systems. You can compile this script into *freemem.exe* (for use by the *freemem* shell script) by typing,

```
cc $DBA/freemem.c -o $DBA/freemem.exe
```

and then setting the execute permission on the file by typing:

```
chmod 700 $DBA/freemem.exe)
```

V

Appendixes

The appendixes contain a series of summary tables showing the Oracle tables and output files created by the scripts described in this book.

SQL Scripts That
Create Oracle Tables

Many of the SQL scripts in this book create tables in the database. This appendix contains a list (see Table A-1) showing the name of each SQL script that creates an Oracle table, along with the name of the table created. Note that tables will be created in the user's schema. Some tables are temporary, and therefore are removed at the end of a script execution; these are normally indicated by *temp* or *tmp* in the table name.

Table A-1. SQL Scripts and Their Corresponding Oracle Tables

SQL Script Name	Table Name
alertlog.sql	alertlog_temp
analinds.sql	nalinds_temp
analyze.sql	anal_temp
ccontrol.sql	create_control_tmp
cdindex.sql	indx_temp
cindex.sql	cindex_temp
cindex.sql	create_index_tmp
crbodys.sql	body_temp
crclusts.sql	clus_temp
crcomms.sql	comm_temp
crconstr.sql	detail_tmp
creback.sql	c_backu_temp
crfuncs.sql	func_temp
crgrants.sql	g_temp
crindexs.sql	indx_temp
crlinks.sql	l_temp
crpacks.sql	pack_temp
crprocs.sql	proc_temp

Table A-1. SQL Scripts and Their Corresponding Oracle Tables (continued)

SQL Script Name	Table Name
crprofs.sql	prof_temp
crroles.sql	role_temp
crseqs.sql	seq_temp
crsnaps.sql	snap_temp
crsnlogs.sql	snaplog_temp
crsyns.sql	syn_temp
crtables.sql	tabl_temp
crtrigs.sql	trig_temp
crusers.sql	u_temp
crviews.sql	view_temp
ddlcon.sql	detail_tmp
ddlcons.sql	detail_tmp
ddlcons2.sql	detail_tmp
ddlndxs.sql	indx_temp
ddlndxs2.sql	indx_temp
ddltbls.sql	tabl_temp
fixowner.sql	fix_own_temp
grantall.sql	grantall_temp
locate2.sql	location_locate_temp
monitor.sql	monitor_table_temp
readonly.sql	readonly_temp
tablecon.sql	tablecon_temp
tablesp.sql	tablesp_tmp
tablestat.sql	tablestat_temp
tblsize.sql	tbldefb
tblsize.sql	tbldeft
tblsize.sql	tbldefa
tblsize.sql	tbldefc
tblsize.sql	tbldefdef
tblsize.sql	tbldefcon
tblsize.sql	tbldefi
tblsize.sql	tbldefk
tblsize.sql	tblsize_temp
tblsize.sql	tblsize_summ_temp
tblsize.sql	tblsize_totals
tblsizec.sql	tablc_temp
waitstat.sql	wait_stat_temp

B

Tables Created by SQL Scripts

As we mentioned in Appendix A, *SQL Scripts That Create Oracle Tables,* many of the SQL scripts in this book create Oracle tables in the database. Appendix A lists each script and shows which table it creates. This appendix is the complement to Appendix A; it contains a list (see Table B-1) showing the name of each Oracle table created in the user schema and the corresponding SQL script that creates the table.

Table B-1. Oracle Tables and Their Corresponding SQL Scripts

Table Name	SQL Script Name
alertlog_temp	alertlog.sql
anal_temp	analyze.sql
body_temp	crbodys.sql
c_backu_temp	creback.sql
cindex_temp	cindex.sql
clus_temp	crclusts.sql
comm_temp	crcomms.sql
create_control_tmp	ccontrol.sql
create_index_tmp	cindex.sql
detail_tmp	crconstr.sql
detail_tmp	ddlcon.sql
detail_tmp	ddlcons.sql
detail_tmp	ddlcons2.sql
fix_own_temp	fixowner.sql
func_temp	crfuncs.sql
g_temp	crgrants.sql
grantall_temp	grantall.sql

Table B-1. Oracle Tables and Their Corresponding SQL Scripts (continued)

Table Name	SQL Script Name
indx_temp	crindexs.sql
indx_temp	cdindex.sql
indx_temp	ddlndxs.sql
indx_temp	ddlndxs2.sql
l_temp	crlinks.sql
location_locate_temp	locate2.sql
monitor_table_temp	monitor.sql
nalinds_temp	analinds.sql
pack_temp	crpacks.sql
proc_temp	crprocs.sql
prof_temp	crprofs.sql
readonly_temp	readonly.sql
role_temp	crroles.sql
seq_temp	crseqs.sql
snap_temp	crsnaps.sql
snaplog_temp	crsnlogs.sql
syn_temp	crsyns.sql
tabl_temp	crtables.sql
tabl_temp	ddltbls.sql
tablc_temp	tblsizec.sql
tablecon_temp	tablecon.sql
tablesp_tmp	tablesp.sql
tablestat_temp	tablestat.sql
tbldefa	tblsize.sql
tbldefb	tblsize.sql
tbldefc	tblsize.sql
tbldefcon	tblsize.sql
tbldefdef	tblsize.sql
tbldefi	tblsize.sql
tbldefk	tblsize.sql
tbldeft	tblsize.sql
tblsize_summ_temp	tblsize.sql
tblsize_temp	tblsize.sql
tblsize_totals	tblsize.sql
trig_temp	crtrigs.sql
u_temp	crusers.sql

Table B-1. Oracle Tables and Their Corresponding SQL Scripts (continued)

Table Name	SQL Script Name
view_temp	crviews.sql
wait_stat_temp	waitstat.sql

C

SQL Scripts That Create Output Files

Many of the SQL scripts in this book create output files that are written to disk. This appendix contains a list (see Table C-1) showing the name of each SQL script that creates an output file and the corresponding name of the output file created.

File extensions indicate the following file types:

File Extension	File Type
.lis	Printed output file
.lst	Printed output file
.sql	SQL script
.tmp	Temporary file

Table C-1. SQL Scripts and Their Corresponding Output Files

SQL Script Name	Output File Name
alertlog.sql	alertlog.lis
allgrant.sql	allgrant.lst
allprivs.sql	allprivs.lst
alltabp.sql	alltabp.lis
analinds	analinds.lis
analyze.sql	analyze.lis
audhot.sql	audhot.lis
auditobj.sql	auditobj.lis
audittst.sql	audittst.lis
audobj.sql	audobj.lis
audses.sql	audses.lis

Table C-1. SQL Scripts and Their Corresponding Output Files (continued)

SQL Script Name	Output File Name
autoplan.sql	autoplan.lis
bad_cons.sql	bad_cons.lis
ccontrol.sql	cr_%sid.sql
cdindex.sql	cdindext.sql
cdindex.sql	cdindext.sql
cindex.sql	cr_index.sql
cindexd.sql	cindexd.tmp
colgrant.sql	colgrant.lst
copyuser.sql	copyuser.tmp
copyusg.sql	copyuser_col_&1.tmp
copyusg.sql	copyusg.tmp
copyusis.sql	copyusis.tmp
copyusl.sql	copyusl_&&1.tmp
copyustg.sql	copyuser_tab_&1.tmp
copyustg.sql	copyustg.tmp
cr_clusts.sql	cr_clust.sql
crbodys.sql	cr_body.sql
crcomms.sql	cr_comm.sql
crconstr.sql	cr_const.sql
creback.sql	bkup_&1.lst
creback.sql	restore_&1.lst
crfuncs.sql	cr_func.sql
crgrants.sql	cr_grant.sql
crindexs.sql	cr_index.sql
crlinks.sql	cr_link.sql
crpacks.sql	cr_pack.sql
crprocs.sql	cr_proc.sql
crroles.sql	cr_role.sql
crseqs.sql	cr_seq.sql
crsnaps.sql	cr_snap.sql
crsnlogs.sql	cr_snlog.sql
crsyns.sql	cr_syn.sql
crtrigs.sql	cr_trig.sql
crusers.sql	cr_user.sql
crviews.sql	cr_view.sql
dbdelete.sql	dbdelete.tmp

Table C-1. SQL Scripts and Their Corresponding Output Files (continued)

SQL Script Name	Output File Name
dbo_sql.sql	dbo_sql.lst
dbousers.sql	dbousers.lst
ddlcon.sql	ddl_drop.tmp
ddlcon.sql	ddl_create.tmp
ddlcons.sql	ddl_create.tmp
ddlcons.sql	ddl_drop.tmp
ddlcons2.sql	ddl_drop.tmp
ddlcons2.sql	ddl_create.tmp
ddlndxs.sql	ddl_drop.tmp
ddlndxs.sql	ddl_create.tmp
ddlndxs2.sql	ddl_drop.tmp
ddlndxs2.sql	ddl_create.tmp
depend.sql	depend.lst
desctmp.sql	descview.lis
descview.sql	desctmp.sql
discon.sql	disconxx.sql
discon.sql	discon.lis
drop_obj	drop_obj_temp.sql
enacon.sql	enaconxx.sql
enacon.sql	enacon.lis
file_use.sql	file_use.lst
fixowner.sql	fix_own.sql
fixtable.sql	fixed.lis
fixtable.sql	cr_fixed.sql
free.sql	free.lst
gantall.sql	grall_tmp.sql
getgrant.sql	regrant.sql
grant_to.sql	grant_to.lst
grantall.sql	grall.sql
indcols.sql	indcols.lis
invalid.sql	invalid.lst
invalid.sql	invalid.tmp
locate1.sql	location.tmp
locate2.sql	location.lis
locks.sql	locks.lis
makeops.sql	makeops.tmp

Table C-1. SQL Scripts and Their Corresponding Output Files (continued)

SQL Script Name	Output File Name
privlist.sql	privlist.lis
privs.sql	privs1.lis
profiles.sql	profiles.lst
quotas.sql	quotas.lst
readonly.sql	readonly_tmp.sql
roellist.sql	rolelist.lst
rollback.sql	rollback.lis
sesstats.sql	sesstats.lis
tabanal.sql	tabanal.lis
tabanala.sql	tabanala.tmp
tabanalc.sql	tabanalc.tmp
tabanali.sql	tabanali.lis
tabanaln.sql	tabanaln.lis
tabanalv.sql	tabanalv.tmp
tabgrant.sql	tabgrant.lst
tablesp.sql	tablesp.lis
tablsizec.sql	inserts.sql
tablstat.sql	tablstat_tmp.sql
tablstat.sql	tablstat.lis
tblsize.sql	tablsize.lst
tblsize.sql	tblsnap.sql
tblsize.sql	tblspddl.sql
tblsize.sql	tblddl.lst
tblsize.sql	tblsnap.lst
tblsize.sql	tblspddl.lst
tblsize.sql	tblddl.sql
usrs.sql	usrs.lst
validate.sql	validate_&1.sql
waitstat.sql	waitstat.lst

D

Output Files Created by SQL Scripts

As we mentioned in Appendix C, *SQL Scripts That Create Output Files*, many of the SQL scripts in this book create output files that are written to disk. This appendix is the complement to Appendix C; it contains a list (see Table D-1) showing the name of each output file and the corresponding name of the SQL script that created it.

Table D-1. Output Files and Their Corresponding SQL Scripts

Output File Name	SQL Script Name
alertlog.lis	alertlog.sql
allgrant.lst	allgrant.sql
allprivs.lst	allprivs.sql
alltabp.lis	alltabp.sql
analinds.lis	analinds
analyze.lis	analyze.sql
audhot.lis	audhot.sql
auditobj.lis	auditobj.sql
audittst.lis	audittst.sql
audobj.lis	audobj.sql
audses.lis	audses.sql
autoplan.lis	autoplan.sql
bad_cons.lis	bad_cons.sql
bkup_&1.lst	creback.sql
cdindext.sql	cdindex.sql
cdindext.sql	cdindex.sql
cindexd.tmp	cindexd.sql
colgrant.lst	colgrant.sql

Table D-1. Output Files and Their Corresponding SQL Scripts (continued)

Output File Name	SQL Script Name
copyuser.tmp	copyuser.sql
copyuser_col_&1.tmp	copyusg.sql
copyuser_tab_&1.tmp	copyustg.sql
copyusg.tmp	copyusg.sql
copyusis.tmp	copyusis.sql
copyusl_&&1.tmp	copyusl.sql
copyustg.tmp	copyustg.sql
cr_%sid.sql	ccontrol.sql
cr_body.sql	crbodys.sql
cr_clust.sql	cr_clusts.sql
cr_comm.sql	crcomms.sql
cr_const.sql	crconstr.sql
cr_fixed.sql	fixtable.sql
cr_func.sql	crfuncs.sql
cr_grant.sql	crgrants.sql
cr_index.sql	cindex.sql
cr_index.sql	crindexs.sql
cr_link.sql	crlinks.sql
cr_pack.sql	crpacks.sql
cr_proc.sql	crprocs.sql
cr_role.sql	crroles.sql
cr_seq.sql	crseqs.sql
cr_snap.sql	crsnaps.sql
cr_snlog.sql	crsnlogs.sql
cr_syn.sql	crsyns.sql
cr_trig.sql	crtrigs.sql
cr_user.sql	crusers.sql
cr_view.sql	crviews.sql
dbdelete.tmp	dbdelete.sql
dbo_sql.lst	dbo_sql.sql
dbousers.lst	dbousers.sql
ddl_create.tmp	ddlcon.sql
ddl_create.tmp	ddlcons.sql
ddl_create.tmp	ddlcons2.sql
ddl_create.tmp	ddlndxs.sql
ddl_create.tmp	ddlndxs2.sql

Table D-1. Output Files and Their Corresponding SQL Scripts (continued)

Output File Name	SQL Script Name
ddl_drop.tmp	ddlcon.sql
ddl_drop.tmp	ddlcons.sql
ddl_drop.tmp	ddlcons2.sql
ddl_drop.tmp	ddlndxs.sql
ddl_drop.tmp	ddlndxs2.sql
depend.lst	depend.sql
desctmp.sql	descview.sql
descview.lis	desctmp.sql
discon.lis	discon.sql
disconxx.sql	discon.sql
drop_obj_temp.sql	drop_obj
enacon.lis	enacon.sql
enaconxx.sql	enacon.sql
file_use.lst	file_use.sql
fix_own.sql	fixowner.sql
fixed.lis	fixtable.sql
free.lst	free.sql
grall.sql	grantall.sql
grall_tmp.sql	gantall.sql
grant_to.lst	grant_to.sql
indcols.lis	indcols.sql
inserts.sql	tablsizec.sql
invalid.lst	invalid.sql
invalid.tmp	invalid.sql
location.lis	locate2.sql
location.tmp	locate1.sql
locks.lis	locks.sql
makeops.tmp	makeops.sql
privlist.lis	privlist.sql
privs1.lis	privs.sql
profiles.lst	profiles.sql
quotas.lst	quotas.sql
readonly_tmp.sql	readonly.sql
regrant.sql	getgrant.sql
restore_&1.lst	creback.sql
rolelist.lst	roellist.sql

Table D-1. Output Files and Their Corresponding SQL Scripts (continued)

Output File Name	SQL Script Name
rollback.lis	rollback.sql
sesstats.lis	sesstats.sql
tabanal.lis	tabanal.sql
tabanala.tmp	tabanala.sql
tabanalc.tmp	tabanalc.sql
tabanali.lis	tabanali.sql
tabanaln.lis	tabanaln.sql
tabanalv.tmp	tabanalv.sql
tabgrant.lst	tabgrant.sql
tablesp.lis	tablesp.sql
tablsize.lst	tblsize.sql
tablstat.lis	tablstat.sql
tablstat_tmp.sql	tablstat.sql
tblddl.lst	tblsize.sql
tblddl.sql	tblsize.sql
tblsnap.lst	tblsize.sql
tblsnap.sql	tblsize.sql
tblspddl.lst	tblsize.sql
tblspddl.sql	tblsize.sql
usrs.lst	usrs.sql
validate_&1.sql	validate.sql
waitstat.lst	waitstat.sql

Index

About the Authors

Brian Lomasky is a Senior Principal Consultant with Oracle Corporation Consulting Services. He specializes in Oracle database and UNIX/OpenVMS/WinNT operating system tuning, troubleshooting, configuration, backup and recovery, and database auditing. When he isn't busy creating new scripts to solve day-to-day problems for DBAs, he has been a featured speaker at the national IOUG-A and Oracle OpenWorld conferences, as well as at local user groups.

David C. Kreines is the Manager of Database Services for Rhodia, Inc., a subsidiary of Rhone-Poulenc S.A. He has worked with Oracle as a developer and database administrator since 1985 on a wide variety of platforms from PCs to mainframes. He has been a frequent contributor to Oracle user group conferences and publications both in the United States and in Europe, and has served two terms as President of the International Oracle Users Group, as well as ten years on the Board of Directors.

Colophon

Our look is the result of reader comments, our own experimentation, and feedback from distribution channels. Distinctive covers complement our distinctive approach to technical topics, breathing personality and life into potentially dry subjects.

The animal appearing on the cover of *Oracle Scripts* is a beetle (*Euchroma gigantea*), of the Buprestidae family of order Coleoptera. This family is commonly known as jewel beetles or metallic wood-boring beetles. Jewel beetles are some of the most brightly colored insects. They inhabit forests or tropical areas and are found on all continents. In some regions, the large, common, and brilliantly colored jewel beetles are used as body ornaments or jewelry. The larvae of the jewel beetle family are wood-borers, eating their way through various types of trees and other plants.

Beetles comprise the largest order of insects in the world; there are at least 300,000 species of beetles in the world, with estimates ranging to well over a million. Species vary in size from about 0.25 mm to over 170 mm, including some of the smallest and largest of the entire insect population. Beetles have two pairs of wings, the outer of which is hardened into a leathery protective layer. They feed on various plant and animal material, and are found under earth or rocks, wood, bark, fungi, or other ground cover, frequently in rotting vegetation or carrion.

Edie Freedman designed the cover of this book, using a 19th-century engraving from the Dover Pictorial Archive. The cover layout was produced with Quark XPress 3.32 using the ITC Garamond font. The CD design was created by Hanna Dyer. Whenever possible, our books use RepKover™, a durable and flexible lay-flat binding. If the page count exceeds RepKover's limit, perfect binding is used.

The inside layout was designed by Nancy Priest and implemented in FrameMaker 5.0 by Mike Sierra. The text and heading fonts are ITC Garamond Light and Garamond Book. This colophon was written by Nancy Kotary; thanks to Mark O'Brien and Chuck Bellamy for their kind help with beetle identification.

 # More Titles from O'Reilly

Oracle

Oracle PL/SQL Programming, 2nd Edition

By Steven Feuerstein with Bill Pribyl
2nd Edition September 1997
1028 pages, Includes diskette
ISBN 1-56592-335-9

The first edition of *Oracle PL/SQL Programming* quickly became an indispensable reference for PL/SQL developers. This new edition covers Oracle8 and includes chapters on Oracle8 object types, object views, collections, and external procedures. It also covers new data types and functions, and contains new chapters on tuning, tracing, and debugging PL/SQL programs. The companion diskette contains an online Windows-based tool offering access to more than 100 files of source code and documentation prepared by the authors.

Advanced Oracle PL/SQL **Programming with Packages**

By Steven Feuerstein,
1st Edition Oct.1996, 690 pages,
plus diskette, ISBN 1-56592-238-7

This book explains the best way to construct packages, a powerful part of Oracle's PL/SQL procedural language that can dramatically improve your programming productivity and code quality, while preparing you for object-oriented development in Oracle technology. It comes with PL/Vision software, a library of PL/SQL packages developed by the author, and takes you behind the scenes as it examines how and why the PL/Vision packages were implemented the way they were.

Oracle8 Design Tips

By Dave Ensor & Ian Stevenson
1st Edition September 1997
130 pages, ISBN 1-56592-361-8

The newest version of the Oracle DBMS, Oracle8, offers some dramatically different features from previous versions, including better scalability, reliability, and security; an object-relational model; additional datatypes; and more. To get peak performance out of an Oracle8 system, databases and code need to be designed with these new features in mind. This small book tells Oracle designers and developers just what they need to know to use Oracle8 features to best advantage.

Oracle Security

By Marlene Theriault & William Heney
1st Edition October 1998
446 pages, ISBN 1-56592-450-9

This book covers the field of Oracle security from simple to complex. It describes basic RDBMS security features (e.g., passwords, profiles, roles, privileges, synonyms) and includes many practical strategies for securing an Oracle system, developing auditing and backup plans, and using the Oracle Enterprise Manager and Oracle Security Server. Also touches on advanced security features, such as encryption, Trusted Oracle, and Internet and Web protection.

Oracle Design

By Dave Ensor & Ian Stevenson
1st Edition March 1997
546 pages, 1-56592-268-9

This book looks thoroughly at the field of Oracle relational database design, an often neglected area of Oracle, but one that has an enormous impact on the ultimate power and performance of a system. Focuses on both database and code design, including such special design areas as data models, enormalization, the use of keys and indexes, temporal data, special architectures (client/server, distributed database, parallel processing), and data warehouses.

Oracle PL/SQL Built-ins Pocket Reference

By Steven Feuerstein,
John Beresniewicz & Chip Dawes
1st Edition October 1998
78 pages, ISBN 1-56592-456-8

This companion to Steven Feuerstein's bestselling Oracle PL/SQL Programming and Oracle Built-in Packages provides quick-reference information on how to call Oracle's built-in functions and packages, including those new to Oracle8. It shows how to call all types of functions (numeric, character, date, conversion, large object [LOB], and miscellaneous) and packages (e.g., DBMS_SQL, DBMS_OUTPUT).

Oracle

Oracle Built-In Packages

By Steven Feuerstein
1st Edition March 1998
600 pages, Includes diskette
ISBN 1-56592-375-8

Oracle's built-in packages dramatically extend the power of the PL/SQL language, but few developers know how to use them effectively. This book is a complete reference to all of the built-ins, including those new to Oracle8. The enclosed diskette includes an online tool that provides easy access to the many files of source code and documentation developed by the authors.

Oracle Performance Tuning, 2nd Edition

By Mark Gurry & Peter Corrigan
2nd Edition November 1996
964 pages, Includes diskette
ISBN 1-56592-237-9

Performance tuning is crucial in any modern relational database management system. The first edition of this book became a classic for developers and DBAs. This edition offers 400 pages of new material on new Oracle features, including parallel server, parallel query, Oracle Performance Pack, disk striping and mirroring, RAID, MPPs, SMPs, distributed databases, backup and recovery, and much more. Includes diskette.

O'REILLY®

TO ORDER: **800-998-9938** • **order@oreilly.com** • **http://www.oreilly.com/**
OUR PRODUCTS ARE AVAILABLE AT A BOOKSTORE OR SOFTWARE STORE NEAR YOU.
FOR INFORMATION: **800-998-9938** • **707-829-0515** • **info@oreilly.com**

How to stay in touch with O'Reilly

1. Visit Our Award-Winning Web Site

http://www.oreilly.com/

★ "Top 100 Sites on the Web" —*PC Magazine*
★ "Top 5% Web sites" —*Point Communications*
★ "3-Star site" —*The McKinley Group*

Our web site contains a library of comprehensive product information (including book excerpts and tables of contents), downloadable software, background articles, interviews with technology leaders, links to relevant sites, book cover art, and more. File us in your Bookmarks or Hotlist!

2. Join Our Email Mailing Lists

New Product Releases

To receive automatic email with brief descriptions of all new O'Reilly products as they are released, send email to:
listproc@online.oreilly.com
Put the following information in the first line of your message (*not* in the Subject field):
subscribe oreilly-news

O'Reilly Events

If you'd also like us to send information about trade show events, special promotions, and other O'Reilly events, send email to:
listproc@online.oreilly.com
Put the following information in the first line of your message (*not* in the Subject field):
subscribe oreilly-events

3. Get Examples from Our Books via FTP

There are two ways to access an archive of example files from our books:

Regular FTP

- ftp to:
  ftp.oreilly.com
  (login: anonymous
  password: your email address)
- Point your web browser to:
  ftp://ftp.oreilly.com/

FTPMAIL

- Send an email message to:
  ftpmail@online.oreilly.com
  (Write "help" in the message body)

4. Contact Us via Email

order@oreilly.com
To place a book or software order online. Good for North American and international customers.

subscriptions@oreilly.com
To place an order for any of our newsletters or periodicals.

books@oreilly.com
General questions about any of our books.

software@oreilly.com
For general questions and product information about our software. Check out O'Reilly Software Online at **http://software.oreilly.com/** for software and technical support information. Registered O'Reilly software users send your questions to: **website-support@oreilly.com**

cs@oreilly.com
For answers to problems regarding your order or our products.

booktech@oreilly.com
For book content technical questions or corrections.

proposals@oreilly.com
To submit new book or software proposals to our editors and product managers.

international@oreilly.com
For information about our international distributors or translation queries. For a list of our distributors outside of North America check out:
http://www.oreilly.com/www/order/country.html

O'Reilly & Associates, Inc.
101 Morris Street, Sebastopol, CA 95472 USA
TEL 707-829-0515 or 800-998-9938
(6am to 5pm PST)
FAX 707-829-0104

O'REILLY®

International Distributors

UK, EUROPE, MIDDLE EAST AND NORTHERN AFRICA (EXCEPT FRANCE, GERMANY, SWITZERLAND, & AUSTRIA)

INQUIRIES
International Thomson Publishing Europe
Berkshire House
168-173 High Holborn
London WC1V 7AA
United Kingdom
Tel: 44-1-71-497-1422
Fax: 44-1-71-497-1426

ORDERS
International Thomson Publishing Services, Ltd.
Cheriton House, North Way
Andover, Hampshire SP10 5BE
United Kingdom
Tel: 44-1-264-342-832 (UK)
Tel: 44-1-264-342-806 (outside UK)
Fax: 44-1-264-364-418 (UK)
Fax: 44-1-264-342-761 (outside UK)
Email: itpint@itps.co.uk

FRANCE
GEODIF
61, Bd Saint-Germain
75240 Paris Cedex 05, France
Tel: 33-1-44-41-46-16 (French books)
Tel: 33-1-44-41-11-87 (English books)
Fax: 33-1-44-41-11-44
Email: distribution@eyrolles.com

ORDERS
SODIS
128, av.du Mal de Lattre de Tassigny
77403 Lagny Cédex, France
Tel: 33-1-60-07-82-00
Fax: 33-1-64-30-32-27

INQUIRIES
Éditions O'Reilly
18 rue Séguier
75006 Paris, France
Tel: 33-1-40-51-52-30
Fax: 33-1-40-51-52-31
Email: france@editions-oreilly.fr

GERMANY, SWITZERLAND, AUSTRIA

INQUIRIES
O'Reilly Verlag
Balthasarstr. 81
D-50670 Köln, Germany
Tel: 49-221-973160-0
Fax: 49-221-973160-8
Email: anfragen@oreilly.de

ORDERS
International Thomson Publishing
Königswinterer Straße 418
53227 Bonn, Germany
Tel: 49-228-970240
Fax: 49-228-441342
Email: order@oreilly.de

CANADA (FRENCH LANGUAGE BOOKS)
Les Éditions Flammarion ltée
375, Avenue Laurier Ouest
Montréal (Québec) H2V 2K3
Tel: 00-1-514-277-8807
Fax: 00-1-514-278-2085
Email: info@flammarion.qc.ca

HONG KONG
City Discount Subscription Service, Ltd.
Unit D, 3rd Floor, Yan's Tower
27 Wong Chuk Hang Road
Aberdeen, Hong Kong
Tel: 852-2580-3539
Fax: 852-2580-6463
Email: citydis@ppn.com.hk

KOREA
Hanbit Media, Inc.
Sonyoung Bldg. 202
Yeksam-dong 736-36
Kangnam-ku
Seoul, Korea
Tel: 822-554-9610
Fax: 822-556-0363
Email: hant93@chollian.dacom.co.kr

SINGAPORE, MALAYSIA, THAILAND
Addison-Wesley Longman Singapore Pte., Ltd.
25 First Lok Yang Road
Singapore 629734
Tel: 65-268-2666
Fax: 65-268-7023
Email: Daniel.Loh@awl.com.sg

PHILIPPINES
Mutual Books, Inc.
429-D Shaw Boulevard
Mandaluyong City, Metro
Manila, Philippines
Tel: 632-725-7538
Fax: 632-721-3056
Email: mbikikog@mnl.sequel.net

TAIWAN
O'Reilly Taiwan
No. 3, Lane 131
Hang-Chow South Road
Section 1, Taipei, Taiwan
Tel: 886-2-23968990
Fax: 886-2-23968916
Email: benh@oreilly.com

CHINA
China National Publishing
Industry Trading Corporation
504 AnHuiLi, AnDingMenWai
P.O. Box 782
Beijing 100011, China P.R.
Tel: 86-10-6424-0483
Fax: 86-10-6421-4540
Email: frederic@oreilly.com

INDIA
Computer Bookshop (India) Pvt. Ltd.
190 Dr. D.N. Road, Fort
Bombay 400 001 India
Tel: 91-22-207-0989
Fax: 91-22-262-3551
Email: cbsbom@giasbm01.vsnl.net.in

JAPAN
O'Reilly Japan, Inc.
Kiyoshige Building 2F
12-Bancho, Sanei-cho
Shinjuku-ku
Tokyo 160-0008 Japan
Tel: 81-3-3356-5227
Fax: 81-3-3356-5261
Email: japan@oreilly.com

ALL OTHER ASIAN COUNTRIES
O'Reilly & Associates, Inc.
101 Morris Street
Sebastopol, CA 95472 USA
Tel: 707-829-0515
Fax: 707-829-0104
Email: order@oreilly.com

AUSTRALIA
WoodsLane Pty., Ltd.
7/5 Vuko Place
Warriewood NSW 2102
Australia
Tel: 61-2-9970-5111
Fax: 61-2-9970-5002
Email: info@woodslane.com.au

NEW ZEALAND
Woodslane New Zealand, Ltd.
21 Cooks Street (P.O. Box 575)
Waganui, New Zealand
Tel: 64-6-347-6543
Fax: 64-6-345-4840
Email: info@woodslane.com.au

SOUTH AFRICA
International Thomson South Africa
Building 18, Constantia Park
138 Sixteenth Road
(P.O. Box 2459)
Halfway House, 1685 South Africa
Tel: 27-11-805-4819
Fax: 27-11-805-3648

LATIN AMERICA
McGraw-Hill Interamericana
Editores, S.A. de C.V.
Cedro No. 512
Col. Atlampa
06450, Mexico, D.F.
Tel: 52-5-547-6777
Fax: 52-5-547-3336
Email: mcgraw-hill@infosel.net.mx

O'REILLY WOULD LIKE TO HEAR FROM YOU

Nineteenth century wood engraving
of a bear from the O'Reilly &
Associates Nutshell Handbook®
Using & Managing UUCP.

POST CARD

BUSINESS REPLY MAIL
FIRST CLASS MAIL   PERMIT NO. 80   SEBASTOPOL, CA

Postage will be paid by addressee

O'Reilly & Associates, Inc.
101 Morris Street
Sebastopol, CA 95472-9902